Sweet Knits

Sweet Knits

30 cute designs for kids

Catherine Graham-Evans

Photography by Ella Mayfield

BLOOMSBURY

LONDON · NEW DELHI · NEW YORK · SYDNEY

**Dedicated to my everythings, always:
Rupert, Hazel, Esmé and Isla**

First published in Great Britain 2013
Bloomsbury Publishing Plc
50 Bedford Square
London WC1B 3DP
www.bloomsbury.com

ISBN: 978 14081 7194 3

Copyright © Catherine Graham-Evans 2013

A CIP catalogue record for this book is available
from the British Library

Commissioning editor: Susan James
Assistant editor: Agnes Upshall
Copy editor: Jane Anson
Cover design: Eleanor Rose
Page design: Elizabeth Healey

This book is produced using paper that is made
from wood grown in managed, sustainable
forests. It is natural, renewable and recyclable.
The logging and manufacturing processes
conform to the environmental regulations
of the country of origin.

Printed and bound in China

Contents

Introduction

If, like me, you find that knitting, tea and cake are among your favourite things, then you should enjoy this collection of fun, summery knits. Half practical, and half just for fun, I have tried to create a collection of patterns that suggest tea parties, fairy cakes and probably lashings of ginger beer!

I love working with cotton as it gives a beautiful, professional finish, but also because it means that the knitting doesn't have to stop when the weather warms up. All the designs are worked in double knitting (DK) or 4-ply yarn, so you can easily substitute wool for cotton and use the patterns for warmer garments when the sun goes in.

I have tried, whenever possible, to include easier options to the tricky bits in the patterns, so there is something for every ability of knitter, from the raw beginner to the old hand.

I hope you have as much fun knitting the patterns as I did creating them.

Catherine

Getting started

OK, so I shouldn't assume, but I have taken a chance on you knowing how to cast on and off, and how to increase and decrease. If you don't already know these things, don't panic! The very best way to learn is to get someone you know to teach you. It's much easier to be able to watch someone, then do it yourself and ask questions along the way. Should you not know any nifty knitters, the next best thing is to look for a video tutorial on the Internet. I have several on my website at www.yarnlark.co.uk that you might like to try.

A few trickier techniques are mentioned in the book, which may be new to you even if you are an experienced knitter. These are explained in the Techniques section on page 105, although you may prefer to search for a video tutorial online. Likewise, I have included instructions on how to block and sew up your pieces. Apologies to left-handed knitters, as I have described all techniques working right-handed. If you knit left-handed, you will need to adapt my instructions accordingly.

As I have tried to include easier options for some of the more complicated bits in the patterns, it's a good idea to quickly skim-read each pattern before you begin, so you can see where the easier or more advanced options are and choose which one to go for.

Choose a yarn you love, that is the best quality you can afford, and play about with colour combinations. You would be amazed at the difference colours can make to a finished piece. Take a look at the different results in the Stripy-sleeved sweater on page 44. Colour combinations can make the difference between a finished garment being sweet for a baby, fun for a toddler or cool for someone who's growing up fast!

I have used only double-knitting (DK) or 4-ply yarn throughout the book, so that any of the patterns can be made with any DK or 4-ply yarn (see page 122 for US equivalents). Many a time I've taken a favourite book of knitting patterns off the shelf, only to find that the yarn used is a specific brand which is no longer available and has a tension that differs from a standard DK or 4-ply. With this in mind, I set out to design a collection of patterns that could be used for years to come. It also means that you can easily transform them from summer knits to winter woollies by using a snuggly wool, cashmere or merino yarn.

Don't be afraid to play around with the pattern. Just because I've created something with stripes, doesn't mean you have to! Have a look at the Little bird dress on page 50, then download knitter's graph paper from the Internet and have a go at designing a motif of your own to darn onto the front. Or maybe you would like a plain tank top (page 57) with striped edging? Be brave and give it a go!

A little word on tension: the measurements given in these patterns are worked from the tension stated. You need to check that you are working to the same tension by knitting a tension square. This is a small piece of knitting to check that you have the same number of rows and stitches in a 10 x 10 cm (4 x 4 in) square as stated in the pattern. If you have more, you knit a little loosely and need to try a smaller needle (try only going down by the smallest amount possible, so if the pattern calls for 3.25 mm needles, try using 3 mm). If you have more rows and stitches than the stated tension, you should try going up a size (try 3.5 mm rather than 3.25 mm). There are some patterns, such as the bunting, where tension doesn't matter, but if you want a garment to fit well then it's a necessary bother. Only the truly lucky are blessed with 'perfect tension'!

Abbreviations and instructions

2 x 2 rib – a ribbed edge created by working {K2, P2} repeated to the end of the row. On the following row you will need to look at your stitches to see whether to K or P next. If the first two stitches are flat like the right side of stocking stitch, start again with {K2, P2}. If they have a bump across the bottom like the wrong side of stocking stitch, you should start {P2, K2}.

dec – decrease

garter stitch – knit every row.

inc – increase. Make an extra stitch, usually by knitting into the front and then the back of a stitch. On purl rows you should purl first into the back and then the front of the stitch.

inc 1 st ea end – increase one stitch at each end of the row. Make 1 extra stitch in the first and last stitch.

K – knit

{K1, P1} x 2 – knit 1, purl 1, knit 1, purl 1. Any instructions in cursive brackets will be repeated as directed.

K2 tog – knit 2 stitches together. Insert needle through two stitches and knit them as one.

K3 tog – knit 3 stitches together. Insert needle through three stitches and knit them as one.

K3 tog tbl – knit 3 stitches together through back of loop. As for K3 tog, but instead of putting your working needle into the front of the three stitches, put it through the three stitches by entering through the top of the loops and coming out at the bottom on the back of the knitting, essentially knitting into the back of the stitches instead of the front.

knit, dec 1 st ea end – knit the row, decreasing 1 stitch at each end. K1, Sl 1, PSSO at the beginning of the row, work to the last two sts then K2 tog.

M1 – make 1. Increase, usually by knitting into the front and then the back of a stitch. On purl rows you should purl first into the back and then the front of the stitch.

needle method for casting on – work as if you are knitting a stitch, but leave it on the left needle instead of transferring it to the right needle.

P – purl

{P1, K1} rep to last st, P1 – the instructions in cursive brackets should be repeated to the last stitch in the row, which you then purl.

P2 tog – purl 2 stitches together. Insert needle through two stitches and purl them as one.

P2 tog tbl – purl 2 stitches together through back of loop. As for P2 tog, but instead of purling through the front of the stitches, as you normally would, purl through the back. This means you will be inserting your needle (on the back of the work) through the bottom of the two stitches and coming out at the top if your needle holding the stitches is pointing upwards.

P3 tog – purl 3 stitches together. Insert needle through three stitches and knit them as one.

purl, dec 1 st ea end – purl the row, decreasing 1 stitch at each end. P2 tog, P to last 2 sts, P2 tog tbl.

rep – repeat

RS – right side. The smooth side of a piece worked in stocking stitch. Each stitch will look like a little 'V' and when this side is facing you, you need to begin a knit row

Sl 1, K1, PSSO – slip 1 knitwise, knit 1, pass slipped stitch over the stitch you have just knitted.

Sl 1, K2 tog, PSSO – slip 1, knit two stitches together as one, pass the slipped stitch over.

Sl 1, P1, PSSO – slip 1 purlwise, purl 1, pass slipped stitch over the stitch you have just purled.

st – stitch

st st – stocking stitch: knit one row, then purl one row. Repeat.

WS – wrong side. The bumpy side of a piece worked in stocking stitch.

yo – yarn over. On the right side, bring the yarn between the two needles, then over the right-hand needle; on the wrong side, take the yarn over the right-hand needle, then between the two needles.

Sweet treats

Every tea party needs to be overflowing with delicious goodies, and these are good enough to eat! These tasty treats make perfect play food, as they are safe for the smallest of diners and can go in the wash when they have been handled by sticky fingers. There is no need to worry about tension for any of these patterns, as it matters not one bit if they end up a little smaller or larger than mine!

Biscuits

Normally, I would advocate using the best quality yarn you can afford, but this is the exception to that rule. These biscuits look great in the cheapest of acrylics and are a good way to use up all those oddments of yarn you have left over from past projects.

I have not included any information about which brands of yarn I used for the biscuits, as I have no idea! They were all oddments of DK I had around the house, which are so satisfying to use up. I have used 4 mm (US #6) needles to make all my biscuits. In DK they become a slightly larger-than-life version, so if you're going for realism use a 4-ply cotton.

Of course, if you are really serious about making your work top-quality, the only way to do it is to buy lots of packets of real biscuits and get stuck into your research … mmm!

Custard creams

The custard cream is a British classic and no collection of biscuits, knitted or otherwise, would be complete without it. The distinctive diamond shape is worked in stocking stitch with moss stitch surrounding it. You can finish it off by sewing the words 'CUSTARD CREAM' in a different shade within the diamond.

I used 4 mm (US #6) needles and a DK yarn.

• •

Top and bottom

(make two in biscuit colour)

Cast on 15 sts

Row 1 – {K1, P1} rep to last st, K1

Row 2 – Repeat row 1

Row 3 – {K1, P1} x 3, K3, {P1, K1} x 3

Row 4 – {K1, P1} x 3, P4, {K1, P1} x 2, K1

Row 5 – {K1, P1} x 2, K7, {P1, K1} x 2

Row 6 – K1, P1, K1, P9, K1, P1, K1

Row 7 – K

Row 8 – Repeat row 6

Row 9 – Repeat row 5

Row 10 – Repeat row 4

Row 11 – Repeat row 3

Row 12 – Repeat row 2

Row 13 – Repeat row 1

Cast off.

continued on next page

Filling *(pale yellow)*
Cast on 15 sts
Work in st st for 26 rows
Cast off.

To make up

Taking the biscuit filling, with right sides together, sew the cast-on and cast-off edges together, leaving a 3 cm (1 in) opening at one end which you will use to turn the knitting to the right side later.

Make the seam in the centre of the filling so you have two neat edges to poke out from between your biscuit sandwich. Sew up the two end edges. Turn right side out through the opening you left in the centre seam.

Place the filling between the two biscuit pieces, with the right side of the stocking-stitch diamond facing outwards. Using biscuit-colour wool, sew through all three layers: top, filling and bottom.

Using a contrasting colour, sew the words 'custard cream' onto the centre diamond on the top of the biscuit, using the photo as a guide.

Bourbon biscuits

The bourbon is so simple to make, yet looks realistic with just the addition of a few holes on the top and bottom. Choose a rich dark chocolate brown yarn for the biscuit and a paler brown for the creamy filling.

• • • • • • • • • • • • • • • • • • • •

Top and bottom
(make two in dark brown)
Cast on 19 sts
Row 1 - K
Row 2 - P
Row 3 - {K2, K2 tog, yo} x 4, K3
Row 4 - P
Row 5 - K
Row 6 - P
Row 7 - {K2, K2 tog, yo} x 4, K3
Row 8 - P
Row 9 - K
Cast off.

Filling *(light brown)*
Cast on 19 sts
Work in st st for 18 rows
Cast off.

To make up
Taking the biscuit filling, with right sides together, sew the cast-on and cast-off edges together, leaving a 3 cm (1 in) opening at one end which you will use to turn the knitting to the right side later.

Make the seam in the centre of the filling so you have two neat edges to poke out from between your biscuit sandwich. Sew up the two end edges. Turn right side out using the opening you left in the centre seam.

Using dark brown yarn, sew through all three layers: top, filling and bottom.

I used 4 mm (US #6) needles and a DK yarn.

Pink wafers

My personal favourite: I love the way the colour of the pink wafer livens up a whole plate of biscuits. Use a really zingy, hot pink if you have one, with a paler pink for the filling. The wafer texture is created by using moss stitch, with stocking stitch for the filling.

I used 4 mm (US #6) needles and a DK yarn.

Biscuit
(make three in bright pink)
Cast on 19 sts
Row 1 – {K1, P1} rep to last st, K1
Repeat this row 8 more times
Cast off.

Filling
(make two in pale pink)
Cast on 19 sts
Work 9 rows in garter st
Cast off.

To make up
Block each part into a good rectangle. Layer the two pale fillings between the darker pink biscuits.

Sew through all five layers with bright pink yarn. Sew in any loose ends.

Jammy dodgers

These family favourites have a distinctive heart-shaped window to give a peek at the jammy centre. On the knit rows, work all the increases into the front and then the back of the stitch, and on the purl rows work into the back then the front of the stitch, except where the pattern tells you to cast on using the needle method. This is done by working as if you are knitting a stitch, but instead of pulling the stitch off the left needle, you leave the new stitch on the left needle.

I used 4 mm (US #6) needles and a DK yarn.

Biscuit top *(biscuit colour)*
Cast on 7 sts
Row 1 – K
Row 2 – P, inc 1 st ea end (9 sts)
Row 3 – K, inc 1 st ea end (11 sts)
Row 4 – P
Row 5 – K, inc 1 st ea end (13 sts)
Row 6 – P

Row 7 – K1, M1, K5, cast off 1 st, K4, M1, K1 (14 sts)
Row 8 – P5, P2 tog tbl (6 sts)
Turn and work on these 6 sts as follows:
Row 9 – K
Row 10 – P4, P2 tog (5 sts)
Row 11 – K
Row 12 – P4, M1, P1 (6 sts)
Turn, and cast on 5 more sts using the needle method. Cut the yarn but leave these sts on the needle as you will use them later.

Rejoin the yarn to the 7 sts waiting on the other needle. Rejoin to the stitch on the centre edge, not the outside edge, so that you are ready to purl the sts. Continue working on just these 7 sts as follows:
Row 8a – P2 tog, P5 (6 sts)
Row 9a – K
Row 10a – P2 tog, P4 (5 sts)
Row 11a – K
Row 12a – P1, M1, P4 (6 sts)

Row 13 – Sl 1, K1, PSSO, K4, continuing on to the other sts waiting on the needle, tying off the loose end as you go: K1, K3tog, K to last 2 sts, K2 tog (13 sts)

Row 14 – P

Row 15 – K, dec 1 st ea end (11 sts)

Row 16 – P

Row 17 – K, dec 1 st ea end (9 sts)

Row 18 – P, dec 1 st ea end (7 sts)

Cast off.

Biscuit base *(biscuit colour)*

Cast on 7 sts

Row 1 – K

Row 2 – P, inc 1 st ea end (9 sts)

Row 3 – K, inc 1 st ea end (11 sts)

Row 4 – P

Row 5 – K, inc 1 st ea end (13 sts)

Row 6 – P

Row 7 – K, inc 1 st ea end (15 sts)

Rows 8–12 – Work a further 5 rows in st st

Row 13 – K, dec 1 st ea end (13 sts)

Row 14 – P

Row 15 – K, dec 1 st ea end (11 sts)

Row 16 – P

Row 17 – K, dec 1 st ea end (9 sts)

Row 18 – P, dec 1 st ea end (7 sts)

Cast off.

Jammy centre *(bright red)*

Cast on 7 sts

Row 1 – K

Row 2 – K, inc 1 st ea end (9 sts)

Row 3 – K

Row 4 – K, inc 1 st ea end (11 sts)

Row 5 – K

Row 6 – K, inc 1 st ea end (13 sts)

Row 7 – K

Row 8 – K, inc 1 st ea end (15 sts)

Row 9 – K 9 rows

Row 18 – K, dec 1 st ea end (13 sts)

Row 19 – K

Row 20 – K, dec 1 st ea end (11 sts)

Row 21 – K

Row 22 – K, dec 1 st ea end (9 sts)

Row 23 – K

Row 24 – K, dec 1 st ea end (7 sts)

Cast off.

To make up

You may need to pull the rings into shape to make them good circles, then block them. Put all three layers together with the right sides on the outside. Using a length of biscuit-colour yarn, sew a circle just inside the edge with stem stitch, sewing through all three layers, creating a slightly raised edge around the biscuit.

Using the same colour yarn, oversew the edges of the heart-shaped hole. There is no need to go through all three layers here, you can just sew it down to the red filling.

Chocolate digestives

By adapting the jammy dodger pattern you can make a chocolate digestive. Work the biscuit base in a beige colour following the biscuit base instructions for the jammy dodger. Work the top in a dark or light brown, following the instructions for the jammy centre. Block into good circle shapes then sew together.

Party rings

For me, party rings bring back memories of birthday parties as a child. There's something pleasing about the colours and the shape that appeals to children and adults alike, and they certainly liven up a plate of brown biscuits! These knitted party rings look brilliant worked in lurid colours, the brighter the better. Match pink with yellow, orange with purple or any other combination that makes your eyes pop!

· · · · · · · · · · · · · · · · ·

I used 4 mm (US #6) needles and a DK yarn.

Iced top *(yellow, orange, purple or pink)*

Cast on 7 sts

Row 1 – K

Row 2 – P, inc 1 st ea end (9 sts)

Row 3 – K, inc 1 st ea end (11 sts)

Row 4 – P

Row 5 – K, inc 1 st ea end (13 sts)

Row 6 – P

Row 7 – K1, M1, K4, cast off 3 sts, K4, M1 in last st (12 sts)

Row 8 – P4, P2 tog – turn and work on these 5 sts

Row 9 – K

Row 10 – P

Row 11 – K

Row 12 – P4, M1, P1

Turn, and cast on 3 more sts using the needle method (see page 9).

Cut the yarn and rejoin to the 6 sts waiting on the other needle. Rejoin to the stitch on the centre edge, not the outside edge, so you are ready to purl the sts.

Row 8a – P2 tog, P4

Row 9a – K

Row 10a – P

Row 11a – K

Row 12a – Inc in first st, P4

Row 13 – K2 tog, K4, K the other sts waiting on the needle to last 2 sts, K2 tog (13 sts)

Row 14 – P

Row 15 – K, dec 1 st ea end (11 sts)

Row 16 – P

Row 17 – K, dec 1 st ea end (9 sts)

Row 18 – P, dec 1 st ea end (7 sts)

Cast off.

Biscuit base *(light brown)*
Repeat as for the top but work in garter st.

To make up
You may need to pull the rings into shape to block them into good circles and to make them match up. Oversew the edges together.

Using a contrasting colour (purple with yellow, orange with pink, etc.), and using the photograph as a guide, sew on wiggly stripes using the Swiss darning technique described on page 110. Every four or five stitches, make a bigger 'V' that stretches over two of the knitted stitches.

Cookies and cream

These have a moss stitch pattern, and a little oval worked in stocking stitch in the centre where you could sew on the name of your favourite cookies and cream biscuit! This pattern is a little fiddly as the increases are worked in moss stitch.

For an easier option, use the stocking stitch biscuit base pattern from the jammy dodger to make the top and bottom biscuit in dark brown, and use the jammy centre instructions in white to make a creamy garter stitch filling.

I used 4 mm (US #6) needles and a DK yarn.

Biscuit bottom and top *(make two in dark brown)*

Cast on 7 sts

Row 1 – {K1, P1} rep to last st, K1 (7 sts)

Row 2 – Inc purlwise into back of first st, then take yarn to back and work 1 st knitwise into front, {P1, K1} rep to last 2 sts, P1, inc into last st knitwise in front and purlwise in back of st (9 sts)

Row 3 – {P1, K1} rep to last st, P1

Row 4 – Inc knitwise into front then purlwise into back of first st, {K1, P1} rep to last 2 sts, K1, inc into last st purlwise in back and knitwise in front (11 sts)

Row 5 – {K1, P1} rep to last st, K1

Row 6 – Repeat row 2 (13 sts)

Row 7 – {P1, K1} rep to last st, P1

Row 8 – Repeat row 4 (15 sts)

Row 9 – {K1, P1} x 2, K7, {P1, K1} x 2

Row 10 – {K1, P1} x 2, P7, {P1, K1} x 2

Row 11 – {K1, P1} x 2, K7, {P1, K1} x 2

Row 12 – {K1, P1} x 2, P7, {P1, K1} x 2

Row 13 – {K1, P1} x 2, K7, {P1, K1} x 2

Row 14 – {K1, P1} x 2, P7, {P1, K1} x 2

Row 15 – {K1, P1} x 2, K7, {P1, K1} x 2

Row 16 – P2 tog, {K1, P1} rep to last 3 sts, K1, P2 tog (13 sts)

Row 17 – {P1, K1} rep to last st, P1

Row 18 – K2 tog, {P1, K1} rep to last 3 sts, P1, K2 tog (11 sts)

Row 19 – {K1, P1} rep to last st, K1

Row 20 – Repeat row 16 (9 sts)

Row 21 – {P1, K1} rep to last st, P1

Row 22 – Repeat row 18 (7 sts)

Cast off.

Centre *(white)*

Cast on 7 sts

Row 1 – K

Row 2 – P, inc 1 st ea end (9 sts)

Row 3 – K, inc 1 st ea end (11 sts)

Row 4 – P

Row 5 – K, inc 1 st ea end (13 sts)

Row 6 – P

Row 7 – K, inc 1 st ea end (15 sts)

Row 8 – P

Row 9 – K

Row 10 – P

Row 11 – K

Row 12 – P

Row 13 – K, dec 1 st ea end (13 sts)

Row 14 – P

Row 15 – K, dec 1 st ea end (11 sts)

Row 16 – P

Row 17 – K, dec 1 st ea end (9 sts)

Row 18 – P, dec 1 st ea end (7 sts)

Cast off.

To make up

Block all the layers, making sure they are a good circular shape. Sandwich the white filling between the two dark brown biscuit layers with the st st shape in the middle with its RS facing out on both top and bottom layers. Sew through all three layers using dark brown wool.

Sew in any loose ends. If you like, sew on the name of your favourite cookies and cream biscuit in the st st area using a lighter brown yarn.

Cupcakes

These pretty little cupcakes make great play food and can be made up just for fun in any DK yarn, or made to be decorative in luxury bamboo or cotton. Try making them in 4-ply yarn for a delicate fairy-cake size, or in DK for a muffin-size cake. Experiment with mixing and matching the different 'toppings' and icings for lots of different looks. Buttons and beads can also look fabulous as sprinkles and cherries. Why not try making a string of hanging cupcakes in pastel colours for a nursery, or some bright cakes to fill a cupcake stand when it's not in use?

Basic cake case

You will need

★ Any 4-ply yarn and 3 mm (US #3) needles to make small cupcakes
★ Any DK yarn and 4 mm (US #6) needles to make large cupcakes
★ Toy filling
★ Buttons and beads if you choose to add them, although bear in mind that these won't be suitable if the cakes are going to be given to young children

I used Patons 100% Cotton 4-ply and 3 mm needles to make small cupcakes and Sirdar Baby Bamboo with 4 mm (US #3) needles for the large cupcakes.

Cast on 80 sts
Row 1 – {K6, P2} rep to end
Row 2 – {K2, P6} rep to end
Row 3 – {K3 tog tbl, K3 tog, P2} rep to end (40 sts)
Row 4 – {K2, P2} rep to end

Repeat this last row for 8 rows more.

Row 13 – P
Row 14 – P (don't knit - you are changing the direction of your st st)
Row 15 – {K3, K2 tog} rep to end (32 sts)
Row 16 – {P2, P2 tog} rep to end (24 sts)
Row 17 – {K1, K2 tog} rep to end (16 sts)
Row 18 – {P2 tog} rep to end (8 sts)

Cut yarn about 30 cm (12 in) from the knitting and thread through remaining sts on needle. Pull sts off needle and pull tight, fastening the loose end. You will use this long end to sew up the cake case.

Cherry cupcakes

Work the cake case as per the pattern on the left. This one has a separate cake and an icing that dribbles only halfway down it. It is topped with a pink or red cherry.

• •

Cake

Cast on 40 sts

Row 1 – K

Row 2 – P

Rows 3–4 – Repeat rows 1 and 2

Row 5 – {K6, K2 tog} rep to end (35 sts)

Row 6 – P

Row 7 – {K3, K2 tog} rep to end (28 sts)

Row 8 – {P2, P2 tog} rep to end (21 sts)

Row 9 – {K1, K2 tog} rep to end (14 sts)

Row 10 – {P2 tog} rep to end (7 sts)

Cut yarn and pull through last 7 sts. Fasten off.

Icing

Cast on 35 sts

Row 1 – K

Row 2 – P

Row 3 – {K3, K2 tog} rep to end (28 sts)

Row 4 – {P2, P2 tog} rep to end (21 sts)

Row 5 – {K1, K2 tog} rep to end (14 sts)

Row 6 – {P2 tog} rep to end (7 sts)

Cut yarn and pull through last 7 sts. Fasten off.

Cherry

Cast on 4 sts

Row 1 – K into the front and back of each stitch (8 sts)

Row 2 – P into the back and front of each stitch (16 sts)

Row 3 – K

Row 4 – P

Row 5 – K

Row 6 – {P2 tog} rep to end (8 sts)

Row 7 – {K2 tog} rep to end (4 sts)

Cut yarn and pull through last 4 sts. Fasten off.

To make up

Stuff the cherry with a little toy filling and sew it up. Sew up the side edges on the cupcake case, the cake and the icing. Sew the icing onto the cake and the cherry onto the top of the icing. Sew the cake onto the case, leaving a small hole for stuffing. Fill with toy stuffing and oversew the hole.

Add ribbons, beads or buttons as you like.

Swirled frosting cupcakes

For these cakes, follow the case and cake instructions for the Cherry cupcake on page 29. Then make a tube of piped icing, either by following the instructions below or using a French knitting dolly should you happen to have one to hand. If you have neither a French knitting dolly nor double-pointed needles (or if the mere idea of double-pointed needles fills you with trepidation), you can achieve pretty much the same result by casting on 8 sts and working st st until you have enough knitting to make a decent swirl (about 42 cm (17 in) for a DK cupcake or 38 cm (15 in) for a 4-ply one).

Now you simply need to sew up the long edge to form a 'sausage' of knitting and sew it in place on your cupcake. Top with a button, bead or 'cherry' from the previous pattern, or try a strawberry or sugar rose from the patterns on the following pages.

You will need

★ *Two double-pointed needles, 4 mm (US #6) for DK or 3 mm (US #3) for 4-ply, although it doesn't really matter too much if the needle size is a little smaller or bigger*

Swirled frosting

Cast on 4 sts

Row 1 – K

Do not turn the knitting as you normally would, but instead, slide sts to other end of needle. Swap the needles over so the needle with the sts on is in the hand it is usually in when you start a row.

Making sure the yarn passes across the back of your work, K the next row.

Continue like this until you have approx 38 cm (15 in) for a 4-ply cupcake or 42 cm (17 in) for a DK one.

Cut yarn, leaving a long end. Thread this through remaining sts on needle. Pull tight and fasten off.

To make up

Make up the cake and case as per instructions for the cherry cupcake. You will find it easier to sew the swirled frosting onto the cake before attaching the cake to the case, as you can get your fingers inside it. I find it easier to sew the frosting in a swirl as I go along, but you may want to pin or tack it into position first in case you run out of swirl by the time you get to the top! If you do, don't unpick it all! Simply add a cherry, bead or button to cover up the gap.

Sugar roses

These are so simple to make and look beautiful on the top of the cupcakes, although you could easily make lots to sew around the edge of a bag, or around the neckline of a cardigan. I have used the reverse side of the leaves to add a different texture to my cupcakes, but the right side of the stocking stitch gives a smooth effect which looks good too.

I used Patons 100% Cotton 4-ply and 3 mm (US #3) needles, but you could easily use DK with 4 mm (US #6) needles to make larger roses.

Leaves

Cast on 4 sts

Row 1 – K into the front and back of each stitch (8 sts)

Row 2 – P

Starting with a K row, work in st st for a further 6 rows

Row 9 – {K2 tog} rep to end (4 sts)

Row 10 – {P2 tog} rep to end (2 sts)

Row 11 – K2 tog

Fasten off.

Rose

Cast on 30 sts

Row 1 – K

Row 2 – P

Row 3 – {K2 tog} rep to end (15 sts)

Row 4 – P

Row 5 – K

Cut a long end and thread it through all remaining sts. Pull tight but do not fasten off. Instead, thread the end through a needle and, as you pull tight, roll up the knitting in a spiral to form a rose. Secure with a few sts.

To make up

Sew leaves in place and sew the rose in the centre. Roll the outside edge of the rose down a little to look like flower petals opening.

Strawberries

These are brilliant for play food made in DK cotton, as they come out around the size of large, real strawberries. Stuffed with toy filling, they are quick and easy to make, and safe for smaller children, although I hid a jingle bell in the centre of each, which means they are not suitable for tiny ones, but more fun for three-year-olds and over!

When made up in 4-ply on 3 mm needles you end up with smaller strawberries which I have used for a pretty strawberry edging (page 100). By using 4-ply and 2 mm (US #0) needles, I made a perfectly-formed miniature version, which I used to top the cupcakes in the previous patterns.

You will need

★ *Large strawberries: DK cotton on 4 mm or 3.75 mm (US #5) needles*
★ *Small strawberries: 4-ply cotton on 2.75 mm (US #2) needles*
★ *Miniature strawberries: 4-ply or crochet cotton on 2 mm (US #0) needles*
★ *(See Shade chart on page 123 for details of colours)*

Notes

★ *Work all increases by knitting into the front and back of each stitch*
★ *When changing colours it is important to twist the yarns once to ensure no gaps appear in your work*

Abbreviations

K1r / P1r – knit or purl using red yarn
K1g / P1g – knit or purl using green yarn

Strawberry *(red)*

Cast on 4 sts
Row 1 – M1 in each stitch (8 sts)
Row 2 – P
Row 3 – M1 in each stitch (16 sts)
Row 4 – P
Row 5 – M1 in each stitch (32 sts)
Row 6 – P
Row 7 – K
Row 8 – P
Attach green yarn and work as follows, changing colours as directed:
Row 9 – K1r, {K2r, K1g, K2r} rep 5 more times, K1r
Row 10 – P1r, {P1r, P3g, P1r} rep 5 more times, P1r

Row 11 – Using green from here on, K2 tog to end (16 sts)
Row 12 – P2 tog to end (8 sts)
Row 13 – K2 tog to end (4 sts)
Row 14 – P
Row 15 – K
Row 16 – P
Cut a long end and thread yarn through remaining sts on needle. Pull tight and fasten off.

To make up

Sew edges together, stuffing with toy filling just before you close up the strawberry. With green yarn, sew edges of stem together to make a tube. Close up the end. If any gaps appear where your knitting is a bit loose, you can sew these up with a stitch.

Using yellow yarn, sew a scattering of v-shaped stitches over the strawberry to look like seeds, using the Swiss darning technique described on page 110.

Fairy blossom tea set

Every tea party needs a tea set and this quirky little tea set is perfect for small hands. The three 'leaves' which act as the calyx of each flower keep the cups rigid and enable them to be 'hollow' like a real tea set. If you don't want your cups to be flowers, you can stiffen them with fabric stiffener to achieve the same effect. Make it, as I have done, to resemble fairy flowers, or mix it up with mismatching pastels or brights. Why not try knitting it up in red and adding lots of tiny white buttons for polka dots.

You will need

★ 3 mm (US #3) needles
★ 100% cotton DK yarn. Don't be tempted to use wool or acrylic yarn as it really needs to be cotton. You could use 4-ply to make a smaller version of the teapot, but you would need to adjust your needle size accordingly and use the smallest needles you can find.
★ Fabric stiffener
★ Thin wire
★ Buttons (approx. 2 cm / 0.75 in diameter): 2 for the teapot and 2 for each cup
★ Toy stuffing or cotton wool

Notes

★ If you want your teapot to be solid, then make all increases by working into the front then back of each stitch on a knit row, and the back then front of each stitch on a purl row. However, if you choose to make stitches by picking up the thread lying between the two loops (the one you have just knitted and the one you are about to knit), this will make a pretty holey pattern in your tea set (see page 39).
★ Make sure you work any increases in the handle and spout into the front and back of the stitch though, as you don't want holes in these!

Row 3 - K1 {K3tog tbl, K3 tog, K2} repeat to last 7 sts, K3tog tbl, K3 tog, K1 (52 sts)

– Work in st st for a further 3 rows

Row 7 - K1, {K2 tog, K2} rep to last 3 sts, K2 tog, K1 (39 sts)

– Work in st st for a further 3 rows

Row 11 - K.

Teapot

Top frill

Using 3 mm (US #3) needles, cast on 104 sts (in green for the flower version, or any other colour if you would like the frill to be a different colour from the main body of the teapot)

Row 1 - K

Row 2 - P

Main body

If you are knitting the frill in a different colour from the rest of the teapot, change to the main colour now

Row 12 - K (don't purl – you are changing the direction of your st st)

continued on next page →

– Work a further 5 rows in st st, starting with a P row

Row 18 – K2, {M1, K5} rep to last 2 sts, M1, K2 (47 sts)

– Work a further 5 rows in st st

Row 24 – K2, {M1, K6} rep to last 3 sts, M1, K3 (55 sts)

– Work a further 3 rows in st st

Row 28 – K3, {M1, K7} rep to last 3 sts, M1, K3 (63 sts)

– Work in st st for a further 3 rows

Row 32 – K3, {M1, K8} rep to last 4 sts, M1, K4 (71 sts)

– Work in st st for a further 5 rows

Row 38 – K4, {M1, K9} rep to last 4 sts, M1, K4 (79 sts)

– Work in st st for a further 5 rows

Row 44 – K3, {K2 tog, K8} rep to last 6 sts, K2 tog, K4 (71 sts)

– Work in st st for a further 3 rows

Row 48 – K3, {K2 tog, K7} rep to last 5 sts, K2 tog, K3 (63 sts)

– Work in st st for a further 3 rows

Row 52 – K2, {K2 tog, K6} rep to last 5 sts, K2 tog, K3 (55 sts)

Row 53 – P

Row 54 – K2, {K2 tog, K5} rep to last 4 sts, K2 tog, K2 (47 sts)

Row 55 – P2, {P2 tog, P4} rep to last 3 sts, P2 tog, P1 (39 sts)

Row 56 – K1, {K2 tog, K3} rep to last 3 sts, K2 tog, K1 (31 sts)

Row 57 – P1, {P2 tog, P2} rep to end (23 sts)

Row 58 – {K2 tog, K1} to end (15 sts)

Row 59 – {P2 tog} rep to last st, P1 (8 sts)

Cut a long end and thread through remaining sts on needle. Pull tight and fasten off.

Teapot base

Cast on 36 sts in either main body colour or contrast colour

Work in st st for 8 rows

Cast off.

Teapot lid

Cast on 36 sts

– Work 6 rows in st st

On the seventh row, knit each stitch together with the stitch that is 6 rows directly below it. This will be the cast-on row (see 'Picking up from rows below' on page 106). You will be essentially folding the 6 rows you have worked in half lengthways.

★ *Easier option – If this sounds too complicated, simply cast on 36 sts, work 7 rows and continue as below. When you have finished the lid, fold the cast-on edge under the lid like a hem and sew.*

Row 8 – P

Row 9 – {K4, K2 tog} rep to end (30 sts)

Row 10 – {P3, P2 tog} rep to end (24 sts)

Row 11 – {K2, K2 tog} rep to end (18 sts)

Row 12 – {P1, P2 tog} rep to end (12 sts)

Row 13 – {K2 tog} rep to end (6 sts)

Cut a long end and thread through remaining sts on needle. Pull tight and fasten off.

Teapot lid bobble

Cast on 4 sts

Row 1 – M1 in every stitch (by knitting into the front and back of each stitch) (8 sts)

Row 2 – M1 in every stitch (by purling into the back and front of each stitch) (16 sts)

Row 3 – K

Row 4 – P

Row 5 – K

Row 6 – {P 2 tog} rep to end (8 sts)

Row 7 – {K 2 tog} rep to end (4 sts)

Cut the yarn and pull through the last 4 sts. Fasten off. Stuff with a little toy stuffing and sew up.

Teapot handle

Cast on 4 sts

Row 1 – K1, M1, K to last st, M1, K1 (6 sts)

Row 2 – P1, M1, P to last st, M1, P1 (8 sts)

Row 3 – K1, M1, K to last st, M1, K1 (10 sts)

Work in st st until handle measures 12 cm (4.75 in)

Decrease one st at each end of the next 3 rows

Cast off.

continued on next page ⇨

Teapot spout

Cast on 8 sts

Row 1 – K1, M1, K6, M1, K1 (10 sts)

Row 2 – P

Row 3 – K3, M1, K4, M1, K3 (12 sts)

Row 4 – P

Row 5 – K4, M1, K4, M1, K4 (14 sts)

Row 6 – P

Row 7 – K5, M1, K4, M1, K5 (16 sts)

Row 8 – P

Row 9 – K6, M1, K4, M1, K6 (18 sts)

Row 10 – P

Row 11 – K7, M1, K4, M1, K7 (20 sts)

Row 12 – P

Row 13 – K8, M1, K4, M1, K8 (22 sts)

Row 14 – P

Row 15 – Sl 1, K1, PSSO, K6, Sl 1, K1, PSSO, K2, K2 tog, K6, K2 tog (18 sts)

Row 16 – P

Row 17 – K6, Sl 1, K1, PSSO, K2, K2 tog, K6 (16 sts)

Row 18 – P

Row 19 – K2, Sl 1, K1, PSSO, K2, Sl 1, K1, PSSO, K2, K2 tog, K2, K2 tog (12 sts)

Row 20 – P

Row 21 – K6, turn and work on these 6 sts

Row 22 – Sl 1, P5

Row 23 – K5

Row 24 – Sl 1, P4

Row 25 – K4

Row 26 – Sl 1, P3

Row 27 – K all sts on needle (12 sts)

Row 28 – P6, turn and work on these 6 sts

Row 29 – Sl 1, K5

Row 30 – P5

Row 31 – Sl 1, K4

Row 32 – P4

Row 33 – Sl 1, K3

Row 34 – P all sts on the needle (12 sts)

Row 35 – K

Row 36 – P

Cast off.

Large leaves *(optional – make three for the flower version)*

With 3 mm (US #3) needles and DK, cast on 3 sts and work as follows:

Row 1 – K

Row 2 (and all other alternate rows) – P

Row 3 – {K1, yo} twice, K1 (5 sts)

Row 5 – {K1, yo} rep to last st, K1 (9 sts)

Row 7 – {K2, yo } twice, K1, {yo, K2} twice (13 sts)

Row 9 – {K2, yo} x 3, K1, {yo, K2} x 3 (19 sts)

Row 11 – K1, {K2 tog, yo} x 4, K1 {yo, Sl 1, K1, PSSO} x 4, K1 (19 sts)

Row 13 – K2 tog, {K2 tog, yo} x 3, {K1, yo} twice, K1, {yo, Sl 1, K1, PSSO} x 3, Sl 1, K1, PSSO (19 sts)

Row 15 – K1, {K2 tog, yo} x 4, K1, {yo, Sl 1, K1, PSSO} x 4, K1 (19 sts)

Row 17 – K2 tog, {K2 tog, yo} twice, K2 tog, {K1, yo} twice, K1, Sl 1, K1, PSSO, {yo, Sl 1, K1, PSSO} twice, Sl 1, K1, PSSO (17 sts)

Row 19 – K2 tog, {K2 tog, yo} x 3, K1, {yo, Sl 1, K1, PSSO} x 3, Sl 1, K1, PSSO (15 sts)

Row 21 – {K2 tog} twice, yo, K2 tog, {K1, yo} twice, K1, Sl 1, K1, PSSO, yo, {Sl 1, K1, PSSO} twice (13 sts)

Row 23 – K2 tog, {K2 tog, yo} twice, K1, {yo, Sl 1, K1, PSSO} twice, Sl 1, K1, PSSO (11 sts)

Row 25 – {K2 tog} twice, {K1, yo} twice, K1, {Sl 1, K1, PSSO} twice (9 sts)

Row 27 – {K2 tog} twice, yo, K1, yo, {Sl 1, K1, PSSO} twice (7 sts)

Row 29 – K3 tog, yo, K1, yo, Sl 1, K2 tog, PSSO (5 sts)

Row 31 – K2 tog, K1, Sl 1, K1, PSSO (3 sts)

Row 33 – K3 tog

Fasten off thread through final stitch.

To make up

Sew along the long edge of the teapot main body. Turn the frill back so both the RS of the frill and the RS of the teapot are facing outwards. You can secure the frill with a few stitches if it refuses to lie down nicely!

If you are adding leaves to make the flower version of the teapot, sew these in place now.

With the teapot base, sew long edges together and then short edges together to form a ring. Sew in place on the base of the teapot (over the leaves if you are using them).

continued on next page ⇨

To complete the handle, position one end of the handle just under the frill edge, RS to RS but with the main length of the handle sticking up in the air. Sew the rounded end and about a further 1 cm (0.5 in) of the handle into position. The rest of the handle will fold down over the bit you have just sewn to form the handle. But before you can do that, you will need to add some wire to strengthen it.

Cut a length of wire at least four times the length of the handle. Fold it in half and poke both ends through one of your buttons. From the inside of your teapot, poke both ends of the wire through first the teapot, then the end of the handle you have just sewn. The button should be caught on the inside of the teapot by the wire.

Bend both ends of the wire into a handle shape, using the free length of knitted handle to determine the length. Poke both ends through the teapot where the handle will end and thread the second button onto these ends of wire. Thread the ends

back through a different hole in the button to secure the button. Twist the free ends of wire back up around the wire handle and cover the sharp ends in electrical tape to make sure there is no chance of them poking out. Cover the entire wire handle in a length of thin wadding, wound tightly, and sew the knitted handle over the top of this. Secure the second rounded end of the knitted handle to the teapot.

Sew along the long end of the spout to about halfway down and secure to the teapot on the opposite side to the handle.

Sew the edges of the lid together and attach bobble.

To stiffen the tea set

Put a small plastic bag inside each piece of the tea set. This will prevent the stuffing from sticking to the knitting. Stuff with cotton wool or polyester toy filling. You now need to coat the knitting in fabric stiffener, which is available in haberdashery shops or online.

I used an old spray bottle filled with a mixture of about 2 parts stiffener to 1 part water, as I find undiluted stiffener made the tea set a bit too hard. Diluted mixture strengthens the tea set sufficiently, but keeps it feeling like a textile, although this of course may vary depending on the brand of fabric stiffener you are using.

Spray or soak the knitting and leave it overnight to dry. Make sure you stand the tea set on some foil or a plastic bag to avoid drips of fabric stiffener going everywhere.

Teacups
· · · · · · · · · · · · ·

As with the teapot, choose how you are going to work your increases: picking up the thread between stitches will create a lacy pattern on the cup; working into the front and back of a stitch will create a solid cup.

Using 3 mm (US #3) needles and 100% cotton DK, cast on 80 sts and work as follows:

Row 1 – K

Row 2 – P

Row 3 – K1, {K3 tog tbl, K3 tog, K2} rep to last 7 sts, K3 tog tbl, K3 tog, K1 (40 sts)

Work in st st for a further 3 rows

Row 7 – K1, {K2 tog, K2} rep to last 3 sts, K2 tog, K1 (30 sts)

Work in st st for a further 3 rows

Row 11 – K3, {M1, K5} rep to last 2 sts, M1, K2 (36 sts)

Work in st st for a further 3 rows

Row 15 – K3, {M1, K6} rep to last 3 sts, M1, K3 (42 sts)

Work in st st for a further 3 rows

Row 19 – K3, {M1, K7} rep to last 4 sts, M1, K4 (48 sts)

Work in st st for a further 3 rows

Row 23 – K4, {M1, K8} rep to last 4 sts, M1, K4 (54 sts)

Row 24 – P

Row 25 – K4, {K2 tog, K7} rep to last 5 sts, K2 tog, K3 (48 sts)

Row 26 – P

Row 27 – K3, {K2 tog, K6} rep to last 5 sts, K2 tog, K3 (42 sts)

Row 28 – P3 {P2 tog, P5} rep to last 4 sts, P2 tog, P2 (36 sts)

Row 29 – K2 {K2 tog, K4} rep to last 4 sts, K2 tog, K2 (30 sts)

Row 30 – P1, {P2 tog, P3} rep to last 4 sts, P2 tog, P2 (24 sts)

Row 31 – K1, {K2 tog, K2} rep to last 3 sts, K2 tog, K1 (18 sts)

Row 32 – P1, {P2 tog, P1} rep to last 2 sts, P2 tog (12 sts)

Row 33 – K2 tog to end

Cut a long end and thread through remaining sts on needle. Pull tight and fasten off.

Teacup base

Cast on 20 sts

Work in st st for 4 rows

Cast off.

Teacup handle

Cast on 6 sts

Work in st st until handle measures 11 cm (4.25 in)

Cast off.

Leaves (*optional – make three for each cup*)

With 3 mm (US #3) needles and DK in green, cast on 3 sts and work as follows:

Row 1 – K

Row 2 (and all other alternate rows) – P

Row 3 – {K1, yo} twice, K1 (5 sts)

Row 5 – {K1, yo} rep to last st, K1 (9 sts)

Row 7 – {K2 tog, yo} twice, K1, {yo, Sl 1, K1, PSSO} twice

Row 9 – K2 tog, K2, yo, K1, yo, K2, Sl 1, K1, PSSO

Row 11 – {K2 tog, yo} twice, K1, {yo, Sl 1, K1, PSSO} twice

Row 13 – {K2 tog} twice, yo, K1, yo, {Sl 1, K1, PSSO} twice (7 sts)

Row 15 – K3 tog, yo, K1, yo, Sl 1, K2 tog, PSSO (5 sts)

Row 17 – K2 tog, K1, Sl 1, K1, PSSO

Row 19 – K3 tog

Fasten off through final stitch.

To make up

Sew long edges of teacup together. Follow teapot instructions to attach handle and base ring and to stiffen.

Dressing Up

There's nothing like getting all dressed up for a **summer tea party** or picnic in the park, and this collection of outfits has something for (almost) everyone! All of the patterns have been made up in DK or 4-ply cotton, making them **cool in warm weather**, but cosy enough to cover up when the sun goes down.

Stripy-sleeved sweater

This is a versatile pattern that can be played around with in a number of different ways. I love the way it looks in 100% cotton, but of course it could be knitted in a luxurious wool or cashmere for a winter sweater. You may like to experiment using a cotton for the lower sleeves and rolled neck and hem edges with a wool for the main sweater on top.

I like the way that the appliqué motifs finish the piece and give a different texture, I also think it gives a more 'professional' look, although the 'handmade' look has its own charm. Templates for the motifs I have used are included on page 114, or why not create your own?

One word of caution – check the washability of any fabrics you use – wash and iron them first in case they're going to shrink and include a scrap of white fabric in with the wash so you can see if any colour bleeds. It would be a shame to ruin all your hard work on the first wash day!

I used Patons 100% Cotton for all except the baby sweater, which was Rowan 4-ply Soft. (See Shade chart on page 123 for colours.)

Sizes (cm)	6–12 m	1–2 yr	2–3 yr	3–4 yr	4–5 yr	5–6 yr	6–7 yr	7–8 yr
To fit chest approx.	46	52	56	58	61	64	66	69
Finished length	30	34	36	40	43	47	50	52

Sizes (in)	6–12 m	1–2 yr	2–3 yr	3–4 yr	4–5 yr	5–6 yr	6–7 yr	7–8 yr
To fit chest approx.	18	21	22	23	24	25	26	27
Finished length	12	13.5	14.5	16	17	18.5	20	21

Yarn quantities								
100g balls of 4-ply in A	1	1	1	1	1	1	1	1
100g balls of 4-ply in B	1	2	2	2	2	3	3	3
100g balls of 4-ply in C	1	1	1	1	1	1	1	1

* Please note that these yarn quantities are for the design worked with striped sleeves and a plain body.

★ 1 pair 3.25 mm (US #3) needles
★ 4-ply yarn in three colours: A (rolled neck
   and hem edge), B (main body colour) and C
   (second stripe colour)

Tension
. . . .

★ 28 sts and 36 rows for a 10 x 10 cm (4 x 4 in)
   square

Front

Using 3.25 mm (US #3) needles, cast on 78 (88, 92, 98,
100, 104, 106, 110) sts in A and work as follows:
- K 6 rows in st st (this will form the rolled edge)
- Break yarn and change to B (main colour)
- K
- Work in 2 x 2 rib for 7 rows
If you like to count rows, set your counter to zero
now.
- Work in st st until work measures 18.5 (22, 23, 26,
28, 31.5, 33.5, 35) cm (7.5 (8.75, 9, 10.25, 11, 12.5, 13.25, 13.75)
in), not including the rolled edge. This should be
after 60 (72, 74, 86, 92, 106, 112, 118) rows if you set your
counter to zero after the rib.

Shape armhole

Cast off 3 sts at the beginning of the next two rows
(72, 82, 86, 92, 94, 98, 100, 104 sts)
- Cast off 2 (3, 3, 3, 3, 3, 3, 3) sts at the beginning of the
next 4 rows (64, 70, 74, 80, 82, 86, 88, 92 sts)
- Dec 1 st at each end for the next 4 (6, 6, 8, 8, 8, 8, 10)
rows (56, 58, 62, 64, 66, 70, 72, 72 sts).

Shape neck

Work in st st for the next 16 (16, 20, 20, 22, 22, 24, 24)
rows
- K21 (22, 24, 25, 26, 28, 29, 29), cast off 14 sts, K20 (21, 23,
24, 25, 27, 28, 28). This leaves 21 (22, 24, 25, 26, 28, 29, 29)
sts including the one that was left after casting off
- Turn, and working on just these 21 (22, 24, 25, 26, 28,
29, 29) sts, continue as follows:

– P to last 2 sts, P2 tog tbl (20, 21, 23, 24, 25, 27, 28, 28 sts)

– Cast off 4 sts, K to end (16, 17, 19, 20, 21, 23, 24, 24 sts)

– P to last 2 sts, P2 tog tbl (15, 16, 18, 19, 20, 22, 23, 23 sts)

– Cast off 1 (2, 2, 3, 3, 3, 3, 3) sts, K to end (14, 14, 16, 16, 17, 19, 20, 20 sts)

– Work in st st for a further 8 (8, 10, 10, 12, 14, 16, 16) rows

– Cast off 4 (4, 5, 5, 5, 6, 6, 6) sts purlwise, P to end (10, 10, 11, 11, 12, 13, 14, 14 sts)

– K

– Cast off 5 (5, 5, 5, 6, 6, 7, 7) sts purlwise, P to end (5, 5, 6, 6, 6, 7, 7, 7 sts)

– K

– Cast off remaining 5 (5, 6, 6, 6, 7, 7, 7) sts purlwise. Rejoin yarn to waiting sts and work as follows:

– Cast off 5 sts purlwise, P to end (16, 17, 19, 20, 21, 23, 24, 24 sts)

– K to last 2 sts, K2 tog (15, 16, 18, 19, 20, 22, 23, 23 sts)

– Cast off 1 (2, 2, 3, 3, 3, 3, 3) sts purlwise, P to end (14, 14, 16, 16, 17, 19, 20, 20 sts)

– Work in st st for a further 8 (8, 10, 10, 12, 14, 16, 16) rows

– Cast off 4 (4, 5, 5, 5, 6, 6, 6) sts, K to end (10, 10, 11, 11, 12, 13, 14, 14 sts)

– P

– Cast off 5 (5, 5, 5, 6, 6, 7, 7) sts, K to end (5, 5, 6, 6, 6, 7, 7, 7 sts)

– P

– Cast off remaining 5 (5, 6, 6, 6, 7, 7, 7) sts.

Back
Work as for the front until the start of the neck shaping.

Shape neck
Work in st st for the next 24 (24, 28, 28, 30, 30, 32, 32) rows

– K21 (22, 24, 25, 26, 28, 29, 29) sts, cast off 14 sts, K20 (21, 23, 24, 25, 27, 28, 28) sts. This leaves 21 (22, 24, 25, 26, 28, 29, 29) sts including the one that was left after casting off

– Turn, and working on just these 21 (22, 24, 25, 26, 28, 29, 29) sts, continue as follows:

– P to last 2 sts, P2 tog tbl (20, 21, 23, 24, 25, 27, 28, 28 sts)

– Cast off 4 sts, K to end (16, 17, 19, 20, 21, 23, 24, 24 sts)

– P to last 2 sts, P2 tog tbl (15, 16, 18, 19, 20, 22, 23, 23 sts)

– Cast off 1 (2, 2, 3, 3, 3, 3, 3) sts, K to end (14, 14, 16, 16, 17, 19, 20, 20 sts)

– Work in st st for a further 0 (0, 2, 2, 4, 6, 8, 8) rows

– Cast off 4 (4, 5, 5, 5, 6, 6, 6) sts purlwise, P to end (10, 10, 11, 11, 12, 13, 14, 14 sts)

– K

– Cast off 5 (5, 5, 5, 6, 6, 7, 7) sts purlwise, P to end (5, 5, 6, 6, 6, 7, 7, 7 sts)

– K

– Cast off remaining 5 (5, 6, 6, 6, 7, 7, 7) sts purlwise. Rejoin yarn to waiting sts and work as follows:

– Cast off 5 sts purlwise, P to end (16, 17, 19, 20, 21, 23, 24, 24 sts)

– K to last 2 sts, K2 tog (15, 16, 18, 19, 20, 22, 23, 23 sts)

– Cast off 1 (2, 2, 3, 3, 3, 3, 3) sts purlwise, P to end (14, 14, 16, 16, 17, 19, 20, 20 sts)

– Work in st st for a further 0 (0, 2, 2, 4, 6, 8, 8) rows

– Cast off 4 (4, 5, 5, 5, 6, 6, 6) sts, K to end (10, 10, 11, 11, 12, 13, 14, 14 sts)

– P

– Cast off 5 (5, 5, 5, 6, 6, 7, 7) sts, K to end (5, 5, 6, 6, 6, 7, 7, 7 sts)

– P

– Cast off remaining 5 (5, 6, 6, 6, 7, 7, 7) sts.

Sleeves *(make two)*
Using 3.25 mm (US #3) needles, cast on 52 (54, 56, 58, 60, 62, 64, 68) sts in colour A and work as follows:

– Work 8 rows in st st

– Change to colour C and from this point form stripes by changing between colours A and C every 2 rows

– Work 10 (12, 14, 14, 16, 18, 20, 22) rows in st st

– K, inc 1 st ea end of next row (54, 56, 58, 60, 62, 64, 66, 70 sts)

– Work a further 11 (13, 15, 15, 17, 19, 21, 23) rows in st st

continued on next page →

– K, inc 1 st ea end of next row (56, 58, 60, 62, 64, 66, 68, 72 sts)

– Repeat these last 12 (14, 16, 16, 18, 20, 22, 24) rows 2 more times (60, 62, 64, 66, 68, 70, 72, 76 sts)

– P

– Slip all sts onto a stitch holder (if you are following the easier option below, cast off these sts)

– Now cast on 60 (62, 64, 66, 68, 70, 72, 76) sts using colour B, and work in 2 x 2 rib for 6 rows

– (For an easier option see below) holding the stitch holder behind the left-hand needle, with RS facing you, put your needle through both the first stitch on the needle and the first stitch on the stitch holder. Knit these as one stitch. Continue to knit all the sts, picking up both the needle stitch and the corresponding stitch on the holder behind and knitting them as if they were one. This will join the striped sleeve to the rib and give a false-hem effect with the ribbing. (See 'Techniques' on page 106 for a fuller explanation.)

★ *Easier option – if this seems too complicated, the*
  same effect can be achieved by casting off the sts
  on the holder and sewing them under the ribbed
  part of the sleeve later

– P

– K, inc 1 st ea end (62, 64, 66, 68, 70, 72, 74, 78 sts)
Work a further 7 (7, 9, 11, 11, 11, 11, 13) rows in st st
Repeat the last 8 (8, 10, 12, 12, 12, 12, 14) rows 2 more times (66, 68, 70, 72, 74, 76, 78, 82 sts)
Work a further 0 (2, 0, 0, 0, 0, 2, 2) rows in st st.

Top sleeve shaping

Cast off 3 (4, 4, 4, 5, 5, 4, 4) sts at beginning of next 2 rows (60, 60, 62, 64, 64, 66, 70, 74 sts)

– Cast off 3 (4, 4, 4, 3, 3, 3, 3) sts at beginning of next 2 rows (54, 52, 54, 56, 58, 60, 64, 68 sts)

– Cast off 3 (0, 0, 0, 0, 0, 0, 0) sts at beginning of next 2 rows (48, 52, 54, 56, 58, 60, 64, 68 sts)

– Repeat these last 4 rows (3, 5, 5, 5, 7, 7, 7, 8) more times (12, 12, 14, 16, 16, 18, 22, 20 sts).

For sizes 3–4 yr and 6–7 yr only:
Work 2 further rows as follows:
Row 1 – dec 1 st ea end (12, 12, 14, 14, 16, 18, 20, 20 sts)
Row 2 – P.

For all sizes, continue as follows:
Cast off remaining 12 (12, 14, 14, 16, 18, 20, 20) sts.

To make up

Block all the pieces, then sew up R shoulder seam.

For sizes 6–12 m, 1–2 yr and 2–3 yr only
Pick up and K 16 sts along the left shoulder edge on the front.

Form buttonholes (for easier option see below)

Work 2 rows in 2 x 2 rib starting {K2, P2}

– K2, P2 tog, take yarn to back as if about to knit, yo knitwise, K2, P2, K2 tog, bring yarn to front as if to do a purl st, then yo purlwise, P2, K2, P2

– Work 2 more rows in 2 x 2 rib.

★ *For an easier option simply work 6 rows in 2 x 2 rib,*
  then secure with poppers instead of buttons

Cast off purlwise.

– On the left shoulder edge at the back, pick up and K 16 sts

– P 1 row

– Cast off.

For all sizes, continue as follows:
Neckband

Using 3.25 mm (US #3) needles and colour B (main colour), with RS of work facing you, pick up and K 58 (60, 62, 64, 68, 70, 74, 74) sts evenly around neck front (for the first three sizes, start picking up along the edge of the shoulder rib) and 40 (46, 54, 54, 56, 58, 60, 60) along the neck back (98, 106, 116, 118, 124, 128, 134, 134 sts)

– Work 5 rows in 2 x 2 rib

– Change to A and, starting with a knit row, work in st st for 5 rows
– Cast off purlwise.

To finish
For sizes 6–12 m, 1–2 yr and 2–3 yr:
Lay the front shoulder rib over the left shoulder and sew together where the rib overlaps at the armhole edge only. Sew buttons on the back shoulder under the holes in the shoulder rib.

For sizes 3–4 yr, 4–5 yr, 5–6 yr, 6–7 yr and 7–8 yr:
Sew up the left shoulder seam and neck rib.

For every size
Sew up the side seams and sleeve seams of the sweater. The top shaping edges of the sleeves will have a stepped effect, which will be concealed inside the seam once the sleeve is set into the armhole. Pin the sleeves into the armholes, pulling gently into shape to match the top, bottom and centre points. Sew in place.

Appliqué motif
Choose a motif you would like to use and trace it onto felt or material. Be a bit wary of using fabrics with bright colours that may bleed or shrink. You might like to wash and iron them once before making your motif with them. For the 'Est ...' motif I used felt which I first distressed with a permanent ink. You can choose the year the child was born or an earlier year such as 'Est 1968' for a vintage feel. You will find templates for this on pages 118–119.

Pirate ship
Use the templates on page 120. I used felt for the ship and cotton for the flags.

If using cotton, you will need to iron it onto a piece of fusible interfacing first, to add strength and make sure it doesn't get misshapen when the knitting is stretched. Fusible interfacing will also limit the amount of fraying of the edges, although they will fray a bit. I like that, but if you don't, make sure you cut enough fabric to turn a hem all around the edge of the shape. You can machine-stitch the appliqué to the interfacing if you like at this point, but don't use a sewing machine when attaching the motif to the sweater, or you run the risk of ruining your knitting.

Pin the motif onto your sweater. Sew on by hand with running stitch, using several strands of embroidery thread.

Add details such as a button for the skull and crossbones on the pirate sweater. The bones are sewn on using embroidery thread.

Robot motif
Using the instructions above, cut the following sized rectangles out of fabric with fusible interfacing on the back:
Head – 10 x 13 cm (4 x 5 in)
Face – 8 x 11 cm (3 x 4.25 in)
Body – 7 x 7 cm (2.75 x 2.75 in)
Control panel – 4.5 x 6 cm (1.25 x 2.25 in)
Legs, arms and neck – 1 x 4 cm (0.5 x 1.5 in) – not all of this length will be used for the neck; it will be tucked behind the head and body

Position the rectangles on the sweater using the photograph as a guide. Sew with running stitch and several strands of embroidery thread just inside the edges of each shape. Add buttons to the control panel and for the eyes and antennae.

Little bird dress

This is quite a fiddly pattern, although I have included easier options where I can, but it turns into a beautiful summer dress for a little girl. It could equally be knitted in a wool 4-ply and worn with a long-sleeved t-shirt and tights during the colder months.

The delicate bird design is worked on the front in Swiss darning after the dress is finished, so don't be put off by thinking it's a tricky intarsia motif. (Only the very brave would attempt it in intarsia – so if you're looking for a challenge, feel free!)

You can easily exchange the bird pattern for your own design on the front here if you download some knitter's graph paper.

• • • • • • • • • • • • • • • • • •

I used Patons 100% Cotton 4-ply for all the dresses. (See the Shade chart on page 123 for details of colours.)

Sizes (cm)	1–2 yr	2–3 yr	3–4 yr	4–5 yr	5–6 yr	6–7 yr	7–8 yr
To fit chest approx.	52	56	58	61	64	66	69
Finished length (shoulder to hem):	45	49	52	55	60	65	72

Sizes (in)	1–2 yr	2–3 yr	3–4 yr	4–5 yr	5–6 yr	6–7 yr	7–8 yr
To fit chest approx.	21	22	23	24	25	26	27
Finished length (shoulder to hem):	18	19	21	22	24	26	29

You will need

★ *3.25 mm (US #3) needles (these will need to be long needles)*

★ *3 mm (US #3 or #2) circular needle*

★ *Cotton 4-ply: 2* (3, 3, 3, 4, 4) balls in main colour; 1 ball in contrast colour for all sizes*

Tension

★ *36 rows and 28 sts to a 10 x 10 cm (4 x 4 in) square*

Note

★ *Size 1–2 uses pretty much exactly 2 balls, so although I don't want to tell you to buy an extra ball you may not need, keep in mind that if you leave long ends you may need to buy an extra ball*

Dress front

Using 3.25 mm (US #3) needles, cast on 220 (236, 256, 272, 284, 300, 316) sts and work as follows:
– Work in st st for 12 (12, 12, 14, 14, 16, 16) rows
– (K2 tog) rep to end (110, 118, 128, 136, 142, 150, 158 sts)
– P
– If you like to count rows, set your row counter to zero at this point.
– Work 4 (8, 10, 6, 10, 8, 12) rows in st st
– Continue in st st, dec 1 st at each end of next and every following sixth row, until 72 (78, 86, 90, 92, 96, 98) sts remain
– P 1 row
– This should be 114 (124, 132, 140, 156, 166, 188) rows from where you set your counter to zero.

Shape armhole

Cast off 2 (3, 3, 4, 4, 4, 4) sts at beginning of next 2 rows (68, 72, 80, 82, 84, 88, 90 sts)
– Cast off 2 (2, 3, 3, 3, 4, 4) sts at beginning of next 4 rows (60, 64, 68, 70, 72, 72, 74 sts)
– Dec 1 st at each end of the next 1 (2, 3, 4, 4, 4, 4) rows (58, 60, 62, 62, 64, 64, 66 sts)
– Work in st st for a further 5 (6, 5, 6, 4, 8, 6) rows.

Shape neck

Work in st st for the next 6 (6, 8, 10, 12, 14, 16) rows
– K21 (22, 22, 22, 23, 23, 24). Slip these sts onto a stitch holder, cast off 16 (16, 18, 18, 18, 18, 18), K20 (21, 21, 21, 22, 22, 23). This leaves 21 (22, 22, 22, 23, 23, 24) sts, including the one that was left after casting off.
– Turn, and working on just these 21 (22, 22, 22, 23, 23, 24) sts, continue as follows:
– P to last 2 sts, P2 tog (20, 21, 21, 21, 22, 22, 23 sts)
– Cast off 4 sts, K to end (16, 17, 17, 17, 18, 18, 19 sts)
– P to last 2 sts, P2 tog tbl (15, 16, 16, 16, 17, 17, 18 sts)
– Cast off 1 (2, 2, 2, 2, 2, 2) K to end (14, 14 , 14, 14, 15, 15, 16 sts)
– P
– Sl 1, K1, PSSO, K to end (13, 13, 13, 13, 14, 14, 15 sts)
– P

– Work in st st for a further 4 (4, 6, 8, 8, 12, 12) rows

– K

– Cast off 4 (4, 4, 4, 4, 4, 5) purlwise, P to end (9, 9, 9, 9, 10, 10, 10 sts)

– K

– Cast off 4 (4, 4, 4, 5, 5, 5) purlwise, P to end (5 sts)

– K

– Cast off remaining sts purlwise

– Rejoin yarn to waiting sts and work as follows:

– Cast off 5 purlwise, P to end (16, 17, 17, 17, 18, 18, 19 sts)

– K to last 2 sts, K2 tog (15, 16, 16, 16, 17, 17, 18 sts)

– Cast off 1 (2, 2, 2, 2, 2, 2) sts purlwise, P to end (14, 14, 14, 14, 15, 15, 16 sts)

– K

– P2 tog, P to end (13, 13, 13, 13, 14, 14, 15 sts)

– K

– Work in st st for a further 4 (4, 6, 8, 8, 12, 12) rows

– P.

Shape shoulders

Cast off 4 (4, 4, 4, 4, 4, 5) sts, K to end (9, 9, 9, 9, 10, 10, 10 sts)

– P

– Cast off 4 (4, 4, 4, 5, 5, 5) sts, K to end (5 sts)

– P

– Cast off remaining sts.

Dress back

Work as for front to beginning of neck shaping. Form split at back of neck:

– K29 (30, 31, 31, 32, 32, 33) sts; turn and work on these sts only

– Starting with a P row, work in st st for 10 (10, 12, 14, 16, 18, 20) rows

– Cast off 8 (8, 9, 9, 9, 9, 9) sts purlwise, P to end (21, 22, 22, 22, 23, 23, 24 sts)

– K to last 2 sts, K2 tog (20, 21, 21, 21, 22, 22, 23 sts)

Cast off 4 sts purlwise, P to end (16, 17, 17, 17, 18, 18, 19 sts)

– K to last 2 sts, K2 tog (15, 16, 16, 16, 17, 17, 18 sts)

Cast off 1 (2, 2, 2, 2, 2, 2) sts purlwise, P to end (14, 14, 14,

14, 15, 15, 16 sts)

– K

– P2 tog, P to end (13, 13, 13, 13, 14, 14, 15 sts)

– K

– Work in st st for a further 0 (0, 2, 4, 4, 8, 8) rows

– P.

Shape shoulders

Cast off 4 (4, 4, 4, 4, 4, 5) sts, K to end (9, 9, 9, 9, 10, 10, 10 sts)

– P

– Cast off 4 (4, 4, 4, 5, 5, 5) sts, K to end (5 sts)

– P

– Cast off remaining sts

– Rejoin yarn to remaining sts and work as follows:

– Starting with a K row, work in st st for 10 (10, 12, 14, 16, 18, 20) rows

– Cast off 8 (8, 9, 9, 9, 9, 9) sts, K to end (21, 22, 22, 22, 23, 23, 24 sts)

– P to last 2 sts, P2 tog (20, 21, 21, 21, 22, 22, 23 sts)

– Cast off 4 sts, K to end (16, 17, 17, 17, 18, 18, 19 sts)

– P to last 2 sts, P2 tog (15, 16, 16, 16, 17, 17, 18 sts)

– Cast off 1 (2, 2, 2, 2, 2, 2) sts, K to end (14, 14, 14, 14, 15, 15, 16 sts)

– P

– K2 tog, K to end (13, 13, 13, 13, 14, 14, 15 sts)

– P

– Work in st st for a further 0 (0, 2, 4, 4, 8, 8) rows

– K

– Cast off 4 (4, 4, 4, 4, 4, 5) sts purlwise, P to end (9, 9, 9, 9, 10, 10, 10 sts)

– K

– Cast off 4 (4, 4, 4, 5, 5, 5) sts purlwise, P to end (5 sts)

– K

– Cast off remaining sts.

Armhole edging

Block front and back sides.

Sew together the shoulder seams but do not yet sew together the side seams.

Using a 3 mm (US #3 or #2) circular needle, and

continued on next page ⇨

with RS facing you, pick up and K 38 (38, 40, 46, 46, 54, 54) sts along each armhole edge of front and back (76, 76, 80, 92, 92, 108, 108 sts total)

Work 7 rows in st st

In the next row (easier option below), as you go along, pick up the original stitch you picked up below the 7 rows you have just worked and knit this one and the one on the needle together, casting off the first 14 (14, 15, 16, 16, 17, 17) sts as you make them. This will fold the rows you have just worked back on each other to make a neat edge. (See 'Techniques' on page 106.)

Continue along the row, picking up the stitch from the first row and knitting it with its corresponding stitch on the needle (62, 62, 65, 76, 76, 91, 91 sts)

Cast off 14 (14, 15, 16, 16, 17, 17) sts purlwise (48, 48, 50, 60, 60, 74, 74 sts).

★ *Easier option – If this sounds too complicated, you can simply cast off 14 (14, 15, 16, 16, 17, 17) from the next two rows, fold the knitted edge in half along its length and sew it down*

Both options should now have 48 (48, 50, 60, 60, 74, 74) sts remaining in the centre top of the armhole ready to start the frill.

Shoulder frill

Sl 1, K1, PSSO, {K1, M1} rep to last 2 sts, K2 tog (92, 92, 96, 116, 116, 144, 144 sts)

- P2 tog, P to last 2 sts, P2 tog tbl (90, 90, 94, 114, 114, 142, 142 sts)

- Sl 1, K1, PSSO, {K2, M1} rep to last 2 sts, K2 tog (132, 132, 138, 168, 168, 210, 210 sts)

- P2 tog, P to last 2 sts, P2 tog tbl (130, 130, 136, 166, 166, 208, 208 sts)

- Sl 1, K1, PSSO {K3, M1} rep to last 4 sts, K2, K2 tog (170, 170, 178, 218, 218, 274, 274 sts)

- P2 tog, P to last 2 sts, P2 tog tbl (168, 168, 176, 216, 216, 272, 272 sts)

- Work 4 more rows in st st, dec 1 st at each end

(160, 160, 168, 208, 208, 264, 264 sts)

- Cast off 4 sts at beginning of next 4 rows (144, 144, 152, 192, 192, 248, 248 sts)

- Cast off remaining sts.

Neck edging

Using a 3 mm (US #3 or #2) circular needle, and with RS facing you, pick up and K along the neck edge only, not the sts in the V shape of back split. Start at the left-hand side of the back split, working all around the neck edge to arrive at the right-hand side of the back split.

Row 1 – Pick up and K evenly: 29 (29, 31, 32, 34, 35, 35) sts along back left edge, 62 (62, 64, 68, 70, 74, 74) sts along front, 29 (29, 31, 32, 34, 35, 35) sts along back right edge (120, 120, 126, 132, 138, 144, 144 sts)

Row 2 – P

Row 3 – {K4, K2 tog} rep to end (100, 100, 105, 110, 115, 120, 120 sts)

Row 4 – P

Cast off.

Add the bird detail

Using a brightly coloured cotton, tack a guide line down the centre of the dress, and across the chest where you want the centre of the bird design to be (this will be about 6 (6.5, 7, 7.5, 8, 9, 10) cm (2.25 (2.5, 2.75, 3, 3.25, 3.5, 4) in) down from the start of the armhole shaping).

Using the grid design as a guide, sew on the design in a contrasting colour of 4-ply cotton. If you use the Swiss darning technique, it will look as though the design is part of the knitting.

To make up

Sew down the side seams of the dress. Add a loop and button at the top of the back 'V' to close the neck band. I used a crochet hook to make a chain to use as a loop, but if you don't crochet, a thin ribbon or plait of cotton yarn will work just as well.

Stripy V-neck tank top

A little tank top is great for days when the weather is too warm to wear a sweater but not quite warm enough to go without! The higher neckline gives a modern look to this old classic. It looks really smart on small boys with a shirt underneath, or can be made in pretty colours for a little girl.

The 6–12 m version was knitted in Baby Bamboo (Sirdar) DK, all others were knitted in Patons 100% Cotton DK on 4 mm (US #6) needles.

• • • • • • • • • • • • • • • • • • • •

I used Sirdar Baby Bamboo DK for the smallest tank top and Patons 100% Cotton DK for the rest.

Sizes (cm)	6–12 m	1–2 yr	3–4 yr	5–6 yr	7–8 yr
To fit chest approx.	46	52	58	64	69
Finished length (shoulder to hem):	26	30	36	42	48

Sizes (in)	6–12 m	1–2 yr	3–4 yr	5–6 yr	7–8 yr
To fit chest approx.	18	21	23	25	27
Finished length (shoulder to hem):	10	12	14.5	16.5	19

Yarn quantities

DK yarn (100g balls) colour A	1	1	1	2	2
Colour B	1	1	1	1	1
Colour C	1	1	1	1	1
White (or colour D)	1	1	1	1	1

You will need

★ 1 pair 4 mm (US #6) needles

Tension

★ 28 rows and 22 sts to a 10 x 10cm (4 x 4 in) square

Notes

★ This is for a stripy pattern. For an easier option, work in one colour throughout, or work in one colour but use a contrasting colour for the bottom rib, neck and arm edging

★ To work in a single colour you would need 1 (1, 2, 2, 2*) 100g balls of yarn

★ * Size 7–8 yr uses pretty much exactly 2 balls, so although I don't want to tell you to buy an extra ball you may not need, keep in mind that if you leave long ends, you may need to buy more

Front

Cast on 62 (66, 72, 78, 84) sts in colour A and work 8 rows of 2 x 2 rib

Rows 9 – 36 (46, 62, 76, 90), work in st st, striping as follows:

4 rows of colour A

1 row white

2 rows colour B

1 row white

4 rows colour A

1 row white

1 row colour C

2 rows colour A

1 row colour C

1 row white

Continue this striping pattern throughout.

Shape armhole

Cast off 4 (4, 4, 4, 5) sts, K to end (58, 62, 68, 74, 79 sts)

– Cast off 4 (4, 4, 4, 5) sts purlwise, P to end (54, 58, 64, 70, 74 sts)

– Cast off 3 (3, 4, 4, 4) sts, K to end (51, 55, 60, 66, 70 sts)

– Cast off 3 (3, 4, 4, 4) sts purlwise, P to end (48, 52, 56, 62, 66 sts)

– K1, K2 tog, K to last 3 sts, Sl 1, K1, PSSO, K1 (46, 50, 54, 60, 64 sts)

– P

– Repeat these last 2 rows 2 (2, 2, 3, 3) more times (42, 46, 50, 54, 58 sts).

V-neck shaping

K1, K2 tog, K15 (17, 19, 21, 23) SL 1, K1, PSSO, K1 (19, 21, 23, 25, 27) sts on working needle

– Turn and work on these 19 (21, 23, 25, 27) sts

– P

– K1, K2 tog, K to last 3 sts, SL 1, K1, PSSO, K1 (17, 19, 21, 23, 25 sts)

– P

– K to last 3 sts, SL 1, K1, PSSO, K1 (16, 18, 20, 22, 24 sts)

– Repeat these last 2 rows until 7 (8, 9, 10, 11) sts remain

– P

– Cast off 3 (4, 4, 5, 5) sts, K to end (4, 4, 5, 5, 6 sts)
– Cast off purlwise.

With RS facing you, rejoin yarn to the row in which you turned, joining at the last stitch you made before the turn. Work sts left on needle as follows:
– K1, K2 tog, K15 (17, 19, 21, 23) SL 1, K1, PSSO, K1 (19, 21, 23, 25, 27 sts)
– P
– K1, K2 tog, K to last 3, SL 1, K1, PSSO, K1 (17, 19, 21, 23, 25 sts)
– P
– K1, K2 tog, K to end (16, 18, 20, 22, 24 sts)
– Repeat these 2 rows until 7 (8, 9, 10, 11) sts remain
– Cast off 3 (4, 4, 5, 5) sts purlwise, P to end (4, 4, 5, 5, 6 sts)
– Cast off.

Back

Work as for front until start of V-neck shaping
– K1, K2 tog, K to last 3 sts, SL 1, K1, PSSO, K1 (40, 44, 48, 52, 56 sts)
– P
– Repeat these last 2 rows a further 2 (3, 4, 5, 6) times (36, 38, 40, 42, 44 sts)
– Work in st st for a further 8 (8, 8, 8, 10) rows
– K7 (8, 9, 10, 11), K2 tog, turn and work on these 8 (9, 10, 11, 12) sts
– P
– K to last 2 sts, K2 tog (7, 8, 9, 10, 11 sts)
– Work in st st for a further 7 rows
– Cast off 3 (4, 4, 5, 5) K to end (4, 4, 5, 5, 6 sts)
– Cast off purlwise.

With RS facing you, rejoin yarn to the row in which you turned, joining at the last stitch you made before the turn. Work sts left on needle as follows:
– Cast off 19 sts, K to end (8, 9, 10, 11, 12 sts)
– P
– K2 tog, K to end (7, 8, 9, 10, 11 sts)
– Work in st st for a further 8 rows
– Cast off 3 (4, 4, 5, 5) purlwise, P to end (4, 4, 5, 5, 6 sts)
– Cast off.

Shoulder edging

For sizes 6–12 m and 1–2 yr only:
Pick up and K 10 sts along left shoulder edge on the front
Form buttonhole (for easier option see below)
Row 1 – {K2, P2} rep to end
Row 2 – {P2, K2} rep to end
Row 3 – K2, P2 tog, take yarn to back as if about to knit, yo knitwise, K2, {P2, K2} rep to end
Row 4 – {P2, K2} rep to end
Row 5 – {K2, P2} rep to end
Cast off purlwise.

★ *For an easier option, simply work 5 rows in rib and cast off. Sew poppers under the rib instead of a button. You can sew a decorative button on the top if you like the look.*

On the left shoulder edge at the back, pick up and K 16 sts
Row 1 – P

Row 2 – K
Cast off purlwise.

Neckband

For sizes 6–12 m and 1–2 yr only:
Pick up and K an extra 4 sts along edge of shoulder rib. If you chose the more advanced option of making buttonholes, you should make one more buttonhole on these 4 extra sts in row 3 of the neck rib. Continue as below, but when you get to the last 4 sts of row 3 (the sts along the edge of the shoulder rib) work 2 tog and take the yarn over, then work 2 sts, as you did along the shoulder rib. Continue with rows 4 and 5 as below..

For all sizes:
Sew back and front together at right shoulder seam.
With RS facing you, pick up and K 22 (28, 32, 34, 36) sts down the 'V', 22 (28, 32, 34, 36) sts up the other side of the 'V' and 34 (36, 38, 40, 42) sts evenly along the back neck.

Row 1 – With WS facing you, {K2, P2} all along back neck and into the 'V', but make sure you purl all of the bottom 4 sts going down into the 'V' and the first 4 sts coming up out of the 'V'
Row 2 – Continue to work in 2 x 2 rib, but work the 8 sts in the centre of the 'V' as follows: K3, K2 tog, K3 (7 sts)
Row 3 – Continue to work in 2 x 2 rib, but work the 7 sts in the centre of the 'V' as follows: P2, P3 tog, P2 (5 sts)
Row 4 – Continue to work in 2 x 2 rib, but work the 5 sts in the centre of the 'V' as follows: K1, K3 tog, K1 (3 sts)
Row 5 – Continue to work in 2 x 2 rib, casting off as you work along this row, but work the 3 sts in the centre of the 'V' as follows: P3 tog.

For sizes 6–12 m and 1–2 yr only:
Lay the front shoulder rib over the left shoulder and sew together where the rib overlaps at the armhole edge only. Sew buttons on the back shoulder under the holes in the shoulder rib.

For all other sizes:
Sew up the left shoulder seam and neck rib.

Armhole edging
With RS facing you, pick up and K 78 (84, 90, 96, 106) sts evenly along the armhole
– Work in 2 x 2 rib for 4 rows
– Cast off in rib
– Sew side seams and rib edges together.

To make up
Block the tank top and sew up the sides.

Round-neck tank top

The round-neck version of the tank top follows the
instructions for the V-neck version, with a few simple
modifications. I created a small reverse stocking
stitch border at the bottom to add interest. (See
the note at the end of the pattern.)

• •

**I used
Patons 100%
Cotton DK and 4 mm
(US #6) needles. (See
Shade chart on page
123 for details of
colours.)**

Tension
• • • • • • • •

★ *28 rows and 22 sts to a 10 x 10cm (4 x 4 in) square*

Front
Work as for front of V-neck version until start of
V-neck shaping, then continue as follows:
– K1, K2 tog, K to last 3 sts, SL 1, K1, PSSO, K1 (40, 44, 48,
52, 56 sts)
– P
– Repeat these last 2 rows a further 2 (3, 4, 5, 6)
times (36, 38, 40, 42, 44 sts)
– Work in st st for a further 4 (4, 4, 2, 4) rows
– K9 (10, 11, 13, 14), K2 tog, turn and work on these 10
(11, 12, 14, 15) sts
– P
– K to last 2 sts, K2 tog (9, 10, 11, 13, 14 sts)
– Repeat these last 2 rows a further 2 (2, 2, 3, 3) times
(7, 8, 9, 10, 11 sts)
– Work in st st for a further 7 rows
– Cast off 3 (4, 4, 5, 5) K to end (4, 4, 5, 5, 6 sts)
– Cast off purlwise

With RS facing you, rejoin yarn to the row in which
you turned, joining at the last stitch you made
before the turn. Work sts left on needle as follows:
– Cast off 15 (15, 15, 13, 13) sts, K to end (10, 11, 12, 14, 15
sts)
– P
– K2 tog, K to end (9, 10, 11, 13, 14 sts)
– Repeat these last 2 rows a further 2 (2, 2, 3, 3) times
(7, 8, 9, 10, 11 sts)
– Work in st st for a further 8 rows
– Cast off 3 (4, 4, 5, 5) sts purlwise, P to end (4, 4, 5, 5,
6) sts
– Cast off.

Back
Follow the instructions for the V-neck tank top.
Continue as per the V-neck instructions, with only
one modification: when picking up sts for the
neckband, pick up and K 32 (38, 40, 44, 46) sts evenly
along the neck front and 34 (36, 38, 40, 42) sts evenly
along the back neck. Don't forget to add in your 4
extra sts along the shoulder rib for sizes 6–12 m,
and 1–2 yr.

Pockets

Should you wish to add these pretty gathered pockets, they will add a more feminine touch.
Cast on 12 (12, 16, 16, 16) sts

– K1, M1, K to last, M1, K1

– P

– Repeat these two rows 5 (5, 7, 7, 7) times (24, 24, 32, 32, 32 sts)

– {K2 tog} rep to end (12, 12, 16, 16, 16 sts)

– Change colour at this point if you wish

– P

– P (don't knit, as you are changing the direction of your st st)

– Work a further 6 rows in st st, starting with a K row.

In the next row (easier option below) as you go along, pick up the stitch in the same column that is 7 rows below the one you have just worked. This will be from the first row knitted after the {K2 tog} row. If you changed colour it will be easy to see it as it will be the last row worked in the old colour. Pick up each in turn and knit this one and the one on the needle together, casting off as you go. This will fold the rows you have just worked back on each other to make a neat edge (see page 106).

★ *Easier option – If this sounds too complicated, you can simply cast off, fold the knitted edge over and sew it down*

Position the pocket and sew on. You can add a bow of finger-chained yarn (see page 108) if you like.

Note

For the red, cream and blue version pictured here, I worked the rib in cream, then continued as follows:

Row 1 – P (red)

Row 2 – K (cream)

Row 3 – P (cream)

Extra row – purl (blue)

Row 4 – P (blue – this reverses the st st)

I then continued in st st as per the pattern, not counting the 'extra row' as I needed to add it in order to get the st st back on the right side.
The red stitching around the armholes and neck is added on at the end in back stitch.

Bow dress

This is a cool, yet cute little dress. Made in cotton it makes an easy-to-wear summer dress which can be worn with leggings and a t-shirt if the weather is cooler. It would look gorgeous made in a 4-ply luxury yarn like merino or cashmere to be worn with a long-sleeved top and tights in the winter.

Check the finished length against your child. If you would prefer it longer, add a few more rows before you begin the armhole shaping. Even though the pattern only goes up to age 8, as the dress is so gathered it should fit up to a 10-year-old around the chest, although you would need to adjust the length. For an option to create a swingy tunic-style top for an older girl to wear over jeans, see the end of the pattern.

I used Patons 100% Cotton 4-ply. (See Shade chart on page 123 for details of colours.)

Sizes (cm)	1–2 yr	3–4 yr	5–6 yr	7–8 yr
To fit chest approx.	52	58	64	69
Finished length (shoulder to hem):	45	52	60	72

Sizes (in)	1–2 yr	3–4 yr	5–6 yr	7–8 yr
To fit chest approx.	21	23	25	27
Finished length (shoulder to hem):	17.5	20.5	23.5	28

Yarn quantities: 4-ply yarn (100g balls)

Contrast colour	1	1	1	1
Main colour	2	3	3	3*

You will need

★ *1 pair 3.25mm (US #3) needles*

Tension

★ *36 rows and 28 sts to a 10 x 10 cm (4 x 4 in) square*

Note

★ *' Size 7–8 yr uses pretty much exactly 3 balls, so although I don't want to tell you to buy an extra ball you may not need, keep in mind that if you leave long ends, you may need to buy more*

Dress front

Using 3.25 mm (US #3) needles, cast on 156 (177, 196, 216) sts using contrast colour

- If you like to count rows, set your counter to zero
- Working in st st, K 6 rows in contrast colour and change to main colour
- Continue in st st until work measures 32 (37, 44, 54) cm (12.5 (14.5, 17, 21) in), ending with a WS row so RS is facing you for next row. This should be after 116 (134, 158, 194) rows if working to given tension.

Shape armhole

Cast off 5 sts at beginning of next row (151, 172, 191, 211 sts)

- Cast off 5 sts purlwise at beginning of row (146, 167, 186, 206 sts)
- Cast off 3 sts at beginning of row (143, 163, 183, 203 sts)
- Cast off 3 sts purlwise at beginning of row (140, 160, 180, 200 sts)
- K1, Sl 1, PSSO, K to last 2 sts, K2 tog (138, 158, 178, 198 sts)
- P
- Rep these last 2 rows 3 (4, 5, 6) times more (132, 150, 168, 186 sts)
- K

- P
- {K3tog} 10 (11, 12, 13) times. K72 (84, 96, 108), {K3tog} 10 (11, 12, 13) times (92, 106, 120, 134 sts)
- P
- K10 (11, 12, 13), {K3tog} 6 (7, 8, 9) times, K36, {K3tog} 6 (7, 8, 9) times, K10 (11,12, 13) (68, 78, 88, 98 sts)
- P
- K16 (18, 20, 22), {K3tog} 4 (5, 6, 7) times, K12, {K3tog} 4 (5, 6, 7) times, K16 (18, 20, 22) (52, 58, 64, 70 sts)
- P
- K20 (23, 26, 29), {K3tog} 4 times, K20 (23, 26, 29) (44, 50, 56, 62 sts)
- Work in st st (starting with a purl row) for a further 12 (14, 16, 18) rows.
- Cast off.

Dress back

Cast on 124 (138, 146, 152) sts using contrast colour

- Working in st st, work 6 rows in contrast colour and change to main colour
- K1, Sl 1, PSSO, K to last 2 sts, K2 tog (122, 136, 144, 150 sts)
- Work in st st for a further 5 (7, 5, 5) rows
- Repeat these last 6 (8, 6, 6) rows 6 more times (110, 124, 132, 138 sts)
- K1, Sl 1, PSSO, K to last 2 sts, K2 tog (108, 122, 130, 136 sts)
- Work in st st for a further 3 (3, 5, 7) rows
- Repeat these last 4 (4, 6, 8) rows 17 more times (74, 88, 96, 102 sts)
- K1, Sl 1, PSSO, K to last 2 sts, K2 tog (72, 86, 94, 100 sts)
- Work in st st for a further 1 (1, 5, 7) more rows.

Shape armhole

Cast off 4 (5, 5, 5) sts at beginning of next row (68, 81, 89, 95 sts)

- Cast off 4 (5, 5, 5) sts purlwise at beginning of next row (64, 76, 84, 90 sts)
- Cast off 4 (5, 5, 5) sts at beginning of next row (60, 71, 79, 85 sts)
- Cast off 4 (5, 5, 5) sts purlwise at beginning of next row (56, 66, 74, 80 sts)

– K1, Sl 1, PSSO, K to last 2 sts, K2 tog (54, 64, 72, 78 sts)

– Work in st st for a further 7 (3, 1, 7) rows

– K1, Sl 1, PSSO, K to last 2 sts, K2 tog (52, 62, 70, 76 sts)

– Work in st st for a further 5 rows

– Repeat the last 6 rows 4 (6, 7, 7) times more (44, 50, 56, 62 sts)

– Cast off.

Bow

Cast on 28 (32, 34, 38) sts using contrast colour

– Work in st st until work measures 36 (40, 44, 48) cm (14 (15.5, 17, 19) in)

– Cast off

Block, then with the right sides facing, sew the two short edges together. This will have formed a cylinder with the right sides inside. Flatten this into a rectangle, making sure the seam is in the centre. Sew up the two long edges, turning the work right side out just before you finish sewing. This will be the main section of your bow.

Bow knot

Cast on 28 sts using contrast colour.

– Work in st st until work measures 9 (10, 11, 12) cm (3.5 (4, 4.25, 4.75)) in

– Cast off

Fold in half lengthways, with the right side on the inside. Sew along the long edge. Turn right side out and fold over the centre of the bow. Sew the short edges together to secure.

To make up

Block the front and back of the dress, easing into shape if necessary. Due to the folds on the front of the dress, you won't be able to block it flat, but you will need to block the edges, especially the bottom edge, to ensure it doesn't roll up too much.

You will see where to position the bow on the front of the dress as the shapings mark the correct position of the bottom of the bow. The top of the dress front will come halfway up the bow. Sew the bow in place.

Join the side seams of the front and back. Match the top edges of the back dress to the top edges of the bow. The back dress attaches to the bow and not to the dress front at the shoulders. Sew together for about 2.5 cm (1 in) from the outside edge. On the other side, attach two poppers so the back edge of the dress, which acts as a shoulder seam, will pop to the top back of the bow.

Swingy top option

Front

Cast on 156 (177, 196, 216) sts using contrast colour

– Working in st st, work 6 rows in contrast colour

– Change to main colour and continue in st st until work measures 24 (24, 27, 30) cm (9.5 (9.5, 10.5, 12) in), ending with a WS row so RS is facing you for next row

– Continue from armhole shaping as per dress front pattern.

Back

Cast on 144 (172, 188, 200) sts using contrast colour

– In st st, work 6 rows in contrast colour

– Change to main colour and continue in st st until work measures 24 (24, 27, 30) cm (9.5 (9.5, 10.5, 12) in), ending with a WS row so RS is facing you for next row

– {K2 tog} rep to end (72, 86, 94, 100 sts)

– Continue from armhole shaping as per dress back pattern

Make bow and make up as per dress pattern.

Shrugs

Shrugs are perfect for summer weather as you can throw them on top of anything when the weather gets chilly, and they're easy peasy to make. Basically, you can make a shrug from a rectangle of knitting. You don't have to worry too much about getting a good fit, because they're designed to be loose, and they don't do up, so no worries over chest measurements or fiddly fastenings!

I have included patterns for two variations, but once you have the general idea of how a rectangle sews up to be a shrug you can play about with different lacy knits and edgings.

Lacy shrug

Working with lacy patterns takes a little concentration when you start off, but once you are used to the pattern you are creating and what it looks like, you will find this needs less thinking about. The finished result is worth the extra brain power though, as it turns into a beautiful summer shrug.

I used 100% Cotton DK and 5 mm (US #8) needles. (See Shade chart on page 123 for details of colours.)

Sizes	Finished size	50g balls of cotton
6–12 m	30 x 26 cm (12 x 10.25 in)	1
1–2 yr	35 x 29 cm (13.75 x 11.25 in)	1
3–4 yr	40 x 34 cm (15.75 x 13.25 in)	1
5–6 yr	45 x 39 cm (17.5 x 15.25 in)	1
7–8 yr	47 x 42 cm (18.5 x 16.5 in)	1
9–10 yr	50 x 44 cm (19.5 x 17.25 in)	2
11–12 yr	55 x 49 cm (21.5 x 19.25 in)	2
Adult S	60 x 54 cm (23.5 x 21 in)	2
Adult M	65 x 57 cm (25.5 x 22.5 in)	3
Adult L	70 x 59 cm (27.5 x 23.25 in)	3

You will need

★ 1 pair of 5mm (US #8) needles

Tension

★ 16 sts and 26 rows to a 10 x 10 cm (4 x 4 in) square when working the lacy pattern in DK on 5 mm (US #8) needles

For sizes 6–12 m (3–4 yr, 9–10 yr, adult S, adult L):
Using 5 mm (US #8) needles, cast on 50 (66, 82, 98, 114) sts loosely and work in 2 x 2 rib for 8 (8, 12, 16, 16) rows.

Start lacy pattern
Row 1 – K1 {SL 1, K1, PSSO, yo, K1, yo, SL 1, K1, PSSO, K3, SL 1, K1, PSSO, yo, K4, K2 tog, yo} rep to last 4 sts, K1, SL 1, K1, PSSO, yo, K1
Row 2 (and every other alternate row) – {P6, SL 1, P1, PSSO, yo} rep to last 2 sts, P2
Row 3 – K1 {SL 1, K1, PSSO, yo, K2, yo, SL 1, K1, PSSO, K2, SL 1, K1, PSSO, yo, K3, K2 tog, yo, K1} rep to last 4 sts, K1, SL 1, K1, PSSO, yo, K1
Row 4 – as row 2
Row 5 – K1 {SL 1, K1, PSSO, yo, K3, yo, SL 1, K1, PSSO, K1,

SL 1, K1, PSSO, yo, K2, K2 tog, yo, K2} rep to last 4 sts, K1
SL 1, K1, PSSO, yo, K1

Row 6 – as row 2

Row 7 – K1 {SL 1, K1, PSSO, yo, K4, yo, SL 1, K1, PSSO, SL 1,
K1, PSSO, yo, K1, K2 tog, yo, K3} rep to last 4 sts, K1 SL 1,
K1, PSSO, yo, K1

Row 8 – as row 2.

These 8 rows form the pattern. Continue until
work measures 23 (31, 39, 48, 53) cm (9 (12.25, 15.25, 19,
21) in), ending with a WS row so you have the RS
facing to start the rib.

Work in 2 x 2 rib for 8 (8, 12, 16, 16) rows

Cast off loosely in rib.

For sizes 1–2 yr (5–6 yr, 7–8 yr, 11–12 yr, adult M):
Using 5 mm (US #8) needles, cast on 58 (74, 74, 90,

106) sts loosely and work in 2 x 2 rib for 8 (12, 12, 14,
16) rows.

Start lacy pattern

Row 1 – K1 {SL 1, K1, PSSO, yo, K1, yo, SL 1, K1, PSSO, K3,
SL 1, K1, PSSO, yo, K4, K2 tog, yo} rep to last 12 sts, K1,
SL 1, K1, PSSO, yo, K1, yo, SL 1, K1, PSSO, K3, SL 1, K1, PSSO,
yo, K1

Row 2 (and every other alternate row) – {P6, SL
1, P1, PSSO, yo} rep to last 2 sts, P2

Row 3 – K1 {SL 1, K1, PSSO, yo, K2, yo, SL 1, K1, PSSO, K2,
SL 1, K1, PSSO, yo, K3, K2 tog, yo, K1} rep to last 12 sts, K1,
SL 1, K1, PSSO, yo, K2, yo, SL 1, K1, PSSO, K2, SL 1, K1, PSSO,
yo, K1

Row 4 – as row 2

Row 5 – K1 {SL 1, K1, PSSO, yo, K3, yo, SL 1, K1, PSSO, K1,
SL 1, K1, PSSO, yo, K2, K2 tog, yo, K2} rep to last 12 sts,
K1, SL 1, K1, PSSO, yo, K3, yo, SL 1, K1, PSSO, K1, SL 1, K1,
PSSO, yo, K1

Row 6 – as row 2

Row 7 – K1 {SL 1, K1, PSSO, yo, K4, yo, SL 1, K1, PSSO, SL 1,
K1, PSSO, yo, K1, K2 tog, yo, K3} rep to last 12 sts, K1, SL 1,
K1, PSSO, yo, K4, yo, SL 1, K1, PSSO, SL 1, K1, PSSO, yo, K1

Row 8 – as row 2

These 8 rows form the pattern. Continue in this
pattern until work measures 26 (34, 36, 44, 51) cm
(10.25 (13.25, 14, 17, 20) in), ending with a WS row so
you have the RS facing you to start the rib.

Work in 2 x 2 rib for 8 (12, 12, 14, 16) rows

Cast off loosely in rib.

To make up

Block out to the correct size. Fold knitting in half
so the top ribbed edge meets the bottom ribbed
edge. Sew along the unribbed edge, away from the
ribbing, leaving an armhole gap of 11 (11, 13, 15, 15, 16,
16, 17, 18, 18) cm (4.25 (4.25, 5, 6, 6, 6.25, 6.25, 6.75, 7, 7) in)
from the end of the sewing to the folded edge.

The ribbed edge should fold back along the top
of the shrug behind the neck to fit.

Adult summer shrug

What I love about this pattern is that it's so simple to make that once you've completed the frill, you are just working in stocking stitch until you get to the other frill. This means you can watch television and knit without losing track of the plot (or the pattern!) and you can take your knitting with you on the train without needing to constantly look at the instructions. Although I like a challenge every now and again, I also like to keep one of these 'low maintenance' knits on the go for times when I need to keep my hands busy without engaging my brain too much!

I used Patons 100% Cotton 4-ply and 3.25 mm (US #3) needles. (See Shade chart on page 123 for colours.)

Sizes (cm)	Small	Medium	Large
To fit approx. bust	81–86	92–97	102–107
Finished size of shrug:	58 x 54	61 x 57	65 x 59
Finished sleeve length	45	45	45
Width of sleeve at upper arm	35	38	42
Width of cuff at wrist	21	23	26

Sizes (in)	Small	Medium	Large
To fit approx. bust	32–34	36–38	40–42
Finished size of shrug:	23 x 21	24 x 22.5	25.5 x 23.25
Finished sleeve length	17.5	17.5	17.5
Width of sleeve at upper arm	13.5	15	16.5
Width of cuff at wrist	8.25	9	10.25

Yarn quantities			
(100g) balls of 4-ply yarn	3	3	4

continued on next page →

You will need

★ 1 pair 3.25 mm (US #3) needles

Tension

★ 36 rows and 28 sts to a 10 x 10 cm (4 x 4 in)
    square (in st st)

Main body of shrug

Using 3.25 mm (US #3) needles, cast on 162 (170, 182)
sts

Row 1 – K1 (yo, K2 tog) rep to last st, K1

Row 2 – P

Repeat these 2 rows 9 times more

Continue in st st until work measures 48 (51, 53) cm
(19 (20, 21) in)

Repeat the first 20 rows

Cast off loosely.

Sleeves

Cast on 60 (64, 72) sts

Row 1 – K1 (yo, K2 tog) rep to last st, K1

Row 2 – P

Rep these 2 rows 9 times more

Work 2 (4, 0) rows in st st

Continue to work in st st, increasing 1 st at each
end of next row and every following 8th (7th, 6th)
row until you have 98 (106, 120) sts

Continue in st st until sleeve measures 45–50 cm
(17.5–19.5 in), depending on the length of your arms.
(You will need to subtract about 10 cm (4 in) from
your actual shoulder to wrist measurement.)

Cast off.

To make up

Block the pieces out to the sizes given. Matching
centre points for the sleeve and shrug, sew the
sleeves to the sides of the shrug. Sew up side seams
for the shrug and the underarm seam on the
sleeve. The top frill should fold back on the shrug
when wearing.

Finishing touches

I love little knitting projects that can be finished quickly and look beautiful around the home. There are several bunting patterns in this section of the book that would cosy up your kitchen, or decorate a small person's bedroom.

There are also patterns for accessories, either for your home or for yourself, or things that would make special, handmade gifts.

Spot and stripe bunting

Don't be put off by the spots in the bunting, as I have sewn them all on at the end using the Swiss darning technique (see page 110). The flags themselves are simple to make. I made two-thirds of the total number of flags I wanted in plain colours, then darned spots onto half this number (although you could use the grid and knit the spots in if you're handy at intarsia), I then made up the remaining third, changing colour every two rows to form stripes.

continued on next page ⇨

You will need

★ *1 pair 4 mm (US #6) needles and any DK yarn, although I think this looks best in bamboo or cotton*

Tension

★ *22 sts and 28 rows to a 10 x 10 cm (4 x 4 in) square. (However, tension really doesn't matter when you're making bunting!)*

Finished size

★ *When knitted to given tension: 19.5 cm long by 18 cm (7.5 x 7 in) across the widest point*

For each flag (make as many as you wish)
Using 4 mm (US #6) needles, cast on 40 sts and work as follows:
Row 1 – K
Row 2 – P
Repeat these two rows
Row 5 – K2 tog, K to last 2 sts, K2 tog (38 sts)
Row 6 – P
Row 7 – K2 tog, K to end (37 sts)
Row 8 – P
Row 9 – K2 tog, K to last 2 sts, K 2 tog (35 sts)
Row 10 – P
Row 11 – K to last 2 sts, K2 tog (34 sts)
Row 12 – P
Repeat these last 8 rows until 5 sts remain on the needle (Row 49)
Row 50 – P

Row 51 – K2 tog, K to last 2 sts, K2 tog (3 sts)
Row 52 – P
Row 53 – K2 tog, K to end (2 sts)
Row 54 – P
Row 55 – K2 tog
Pull thread through loop to fasten off.

To make up

Sew in any loose threads. Block the flags or press with an iron if your yarn permits. Using the grid on page 115 and the Swiss darning technique, sew on the spots. (See 'Techniques' on page 110 for how to do this.) If you want to strengthen your flags, you can use fusible bonding to attach a triangle of cotton to the back of each one, but I didn't feel mine needed this.

I used Sirdar's Baby Bamboo DK for the spot & stripe bunting and Patons 100% Cotton DK for the Union Jack bunting.

Space the flags evenly on some pretty ribbon
and sew on to make bunting.

Union Jack bunting

Follow the pattern for the spots and stripes
bunting, but work all the flags in plain blue. I used
Patons 100% Cotton DK with ribbons by East of
India (available through many online stockists).

Block the flags and back with fabric if you
choose to. Sew on ribbons and lace trims using
the photographs as a guide. Space the flags evenly
along a piece of ribbon and sew on.

Daisy chain

These cute little daisies can be used in many different ways. They look great sewn onto a green rug to create a grassy patch for a child's playroom, or can be sewn in a line to make a pretty edging to cardies, blankets, bags – the list is endless. Try using one on its own to make a special party invitation or birthday card. With the addition of their green stalks, the daisies can be made into a chain for pretty headbands, garlands or necklaces. I have created a loop in the end of each stem so that the child can thread the daisies into a chain themselves. The last one in the chain will need to be tied to the first with a piece of thread or ribbon.

This pattern seems a bit fiddly until you get used to it, but once you've practised it a few times you will be able to make daisies without even looking, so it's worth persevering.

I used Patons 100% Cotton 4-ply. (See Shade chart on page 123 for details of colours.)

You will need
. . . .

★ *1 pair 2.75 mm (US #2) needles and 4-ply cotton in yellow, white and green.*

★ *You could experiment with thin crochet cotton and even smaller needles if you want a very delicate daisy chain!*

Daisy centre *(yellow)*
Cast on 24 sts
Row 1 – {K2 tog} rep to end (12 sts)
Row 2 – {K2 tog} rep to end (6 sts)
Cut a long thread and pull it through all remaining sts on needle. Pull up tightly and fasten off.

Daisy petals *(white)*
Attach thread to the beginning of the cast-on sts. Pick up and K the first stitch from the cast-on edge.

Using the needle method of casting on (start as if knitting a normal stitch, but leave the stitch on the left-hand needle and transfer the new stitch from the right to the left-hand needle), make 5 extra sts.

Cast these off immediately.

You will need to pick up and knit the next stitch from the yellow centre cast-on edge to finish casting off the white petal. You will then be left with one stitch on the right needle.*

Put the right needle in your left hand and again cast on 5 sts using the needle method.

Cast off.

Repeat this process 16 more times around the cast-on edge. This will mean you are picking up and knitting 2 in every 3 sts along the cast-on edge.

You should be left with 18 petals.

To finish the final petal, pick up one stitch in the base of the first petal, use it to cast off the last stitch, then cut the thread and pull it through this final stitch to fasten off.

With the long yellow thread that you left, sew up the centre of the daisy.

Daisy stalk *(green)*
Cast on 20 sts
Row 1 – K16, Sl 1, K1, PSSO, yo x 2, Sl 1, K1, PSSO
Cast off.

To make up
Sew the stalk to the back of the daisy centre. Make sure the end with the hole in is the loose end and the other end is sewn to the flower, so that you can thread more stalks through the hole to make a chain.

Little string bag

This pretty little bag is about as simple as it gets. It's made from one rectangle and two handles. I have made it in natural-coloured string because it's stiff and hard-wearing by nature. It has a lovely texture and a smell that reminds me of visiting basket shops on holiday.

Because all string is different, you will have to experiment a bit with which needle size to use. I used 5.5 mm (US #9) needles, but I could equally have used larger ones. Make sure you have enough string to finish your bag, or can easily get more of the same.

. . . .

I added the knitted corsage from page 90 to my string bag, as decoration.

You will need

★ *One pair of needles in a size to suit the weight of your string. I used 5.5 mm (US #9).*
★ *Enough string to complete your bag. I used two small balls.*
★ *Pretty fabric to line your bag (optional)*
★ *Fabric stiffener (optional)*

Tension

★ *My tension was 19 sts and 35 rows to a 10 x 10 cm (4 x 4 in) square, but yours will probably be different*
★ *The bag is basically a rectangle which needs to be roughly 27 cm wide by 35 cm long (10.5 x 13.5 in), but the beauty of this pattern is that it doesn't really matter. Every single bag is going to be unique.*

To make the bag

Cast on as many sts as will roughly leave you with a strip of knitting 27 cm (10.5 in) wide. Bear in mind that it stretches, so if the sts on the needle are around 22 cm (8.5 in) they will probably stretch to about the right size when you get into the swing of the knitting. After a couple of rows, if you're not happy with the size, you can try again.

Work in garter st until your work measures about 35 cm (13.5 in).

Cast off.

To make the straps

Cast on as many sts as you like to make the handles. You will want them about 3–4 cm (1.25–1.5 in) wide. I used 6 sts.

Work in garter st until work measures about 33 cm (13 in).

Cast off.

Make the second in the same way.

To make up

Fold the bag in half, matching cast-on edge to cast-off edge. Sew down the two sides.

Put your hand inside the bag, with one seam running down the centre of your hand, from the tip of your middle finger to the base of your palm. You should have a pointy corner on top of your middle finger. Make a mark or place a pin about 5 cm (2 in) up the seam from the corner. Pinch this corner, and fold it down so the point of the corner rests on the mark you have just made. Sew the corner in place on this mark.

Do the same with the other side. You have created a flat bottom for your bag. Turn your bag inside out. This will now be the outside. Where the base of the bag meets the side there will be a hole which is the inside of the pointy corner you sewed on the inside of the bag. Sew up this hole.

Position the two handles on the outside of the bag, using the pictures as a guide. Sew on the handles.

You can add buttons to your bag on the ends of the straps, or add a knitted corsage. To make a lining in a pretty cotton fabric, cut a rectangle that is 3 cm (1.25 in) bigger all around than your bag. Following the same directions as for making the bag, sew up the lining and sew it into the inside of the knitted bag.

If you find that your bag is not stiff enough on its own, line it with a plastic carrier bag, stuff the bag with toy stuffing and spray with a mixture of at least one part fabric stiffener to one part water. Leave to dry overnight and then remove the carrier bag and stuffing.

Knitted corsage

A knitted corsage can be used to add a flourish to any bag, coat lapel, or hair band. I have added one here to a shop-bought elastic hairband, but it would be simple to knit one.

The flower is made of a smaller circle sewn inside a larger one to create a layered effect. Decorate the centre with beads, jewels, buttons or a cluster of French knots.

I have used DK yarn here, but you can use pretty much any yarn you fancy and you will simply end up with a larger or smaller flower. Make sure you change your needle size accordingly.

I used Patons 100% Cotton DK. (See Shade chart on page 123 for details of colours.)

You will need

★ DK yarn (less than one ball)
★ 1 pair 3.25 mm (US #3) and 4 mm (US #6) needles

Tension

★ Doesn't matter for this project

Outside flower
Using 4 mm (US #6) needles, cast on 160 sts.
Row 1 – K
Row 2 – K1, {yo, K2 tog} rep to last st, K1
Row 3 (and all alternate rows) – P
Row 4 – K1, {yo, K2 tog} rep to last st, K1
Change to 3.25 mm (US #3) needles and continue as follows:

Row 6 – {K2 tog} rep to end (80 sts)

Row 8 – K

Row 10 – {K2 tog} rep to end (40 sts)

Row 12 – {K2 tog} rep to end (20 sts)

Row 14 – {K2 tog} rep to end (10 sts)

Row 16 – {K2 tog} rep to end (5 sts)

Cut yarn and thread through remaining sts. Pull tight and fasten off.

Inside flower

Using 4 mm (US #6) needles, cast on 80 sts.

Row 1 – K

Row 2 – K1, {yo, K2 tog} rep to last st, K1

Row 3 (and all alternate rows) – P

Row 4 – K1, {yo, K2 tog} rep to last st, K1

Change to 3.25 mm (US #3) needles and continue as follows:

Row 6 – {K2 tog} rep to end (40 sts)

Row 8 – K

Row 10 – {K2 tog} rep to end (20 sts)

Row 12 – {K2 tog} rep to end (10 sts)

Row 14 – {K2 tog} rep to end (5 sts)

Cut yarn and thread through remaining sts. Pull tight and fasten off.

To make up

Sew up the edges of the outside flower to make a circle. Repeat for the inside flower. Position the smaller circle inside the larger and secure with a few stitches at the centre. Sew in any loose ends.

Decorate the inside of the flower with beads, gems or clusters of French knots. Sew a brooch back onto the back of the flower to use it as a corsage, or sew onto a hair band.

Cups and saucers bunting

This tea set makes a quirky bunting for a kitchen, but the cups and saucers and teapot can of course be used in lots of different ways. They can be sewn onto a knitted, hand-sewn or shop-bought tea cosy, or used to make a decorative edging for a kitchen hand towel. They would look cute sewn in the middle of a quilted cushion cover for a kitchen window seat, or would make unusual pockets on a dress for a little girl. They are not the easiest patterns as there's a bit of colour changing, but if you aren't happy doing this, an easier option is to add all of colour C at the end using the Swiss darning technique (see page 110). If you were going to do this, then ignore any changes to colour C, carry on in whichever colour you are using, and sew on the detail later, using the picture as a guide.

I used Sirdar's Baby Bamboo and 4 mm (US #6) needles. (See Shade chart on page 123 for details of colours.)

You will need

★ One pair of 4 mm (US #6) needles
★ A ball of DK yarn in each colour you wish to use
★ A length of ric-rac, tape or ribbon, as long as you want your bunting to be
★ Fusible interfacing
★ Backing fabric

Tension

★ 22 st and 28 rows to a 10 x 10 cm (4 x 4 in) square

Finished size
. . . .

★ Approx 12 x 14 cm (4.75 x 5.5 in) when made with
   DK and 4 mm needles (US #6).

Work the increases by knitting into the front then
the back of each stitch, or by purling into the back
then the front on purl rows.

   Colours A and B will form the stripes on the
teapot. Colour B will also form the spout and
handle. Colour C should be black, brown or grey for
the space between the pot and handle.

   For smaller areas such as the spout etc., it is
easier to use a little ball of the appropriate colour
rather than carrying the thread across the back.

Teapot
Cast on 17 sts in colour A and work as follows:

Row 1 – K

Row 2 – P1, M1, P to last st, M1, P1 (19 sts)

Row 3 – (switch to colour B and hereafter change
colours every 2 rows unless colour (A) or (B) is
stated) – K

Row 4 – P1, M1, P to last st, M1, P1 (21 sts)

Row 5 – K

Row 6 – P1, M1, P to last st, M1, P1 (23 sts)

Row 7 – In B, cast on 2 sts, K to end (25 sts)

Row 8 – In B, cast on 2 sts purlwise, P to last st, M1
in last st (28 sts)

Row 9 – In B, M1, K3, change to A, K to last 2 sts,
change to B, K1, inc in last st (30 sts)

Row 10 – In B, M1, P3, change to A, P to last 4 sts,
change to B, P3, inc in last st (32 sts)

Row 11 – In B, K to last st. M1, K1 (33 sts)

Row 12 – In B, P to last 5 sts, P2 in colour C, P3 in B

Row 13 – In B, K3. In C, K2. Switch to A, K to last 5 sts.
In B, K5

Row 14 – In B, P5. In A, P to last 5 sts. In C, P2. In B, P3

Row 15 – In B, K3. In C, K2. In B, K to end

Row 16 – In B, P to last 5 sts, P2 in C, P3 in B

Row 17 – In B, K5, cutting and tying C as you go.
Switch to A, K to last 5 sts, switch to B, K5

Row 18 – In B, P5

Turn and work on these 5 sts as follows:
K4, M1 in last st, K1
P to end
Cast off.

Continue on the remaining 28 sts on the needle as
follows:

Row 18 – In A, cast off 1 st purlwise, P to last 5 sts,
switch to B, P5 (27 sts)

Row 19 – In B, K to end

Row 20 – In B, P2 tog, P to last 2 sts, P2 tog (25 sts)

Row 21 – In B, cast off 5 sts, K6, switch to A, K6,
switch to B, K7 (20 sts)

Row 22 – In B, P2 tog, P3, switch to A, P10, switch to
B, P3, P2 tog (18 sts)

Row 23 – In B, K2 tog, switch to A, K to last 2 sts,
change to B, K2 tog (16 sts)

Row 24 – In A, P2 tog, P4. In B, P4. In A, P4, P2 tog (14
sts)

Row 25 – In A, K2 tog, K2. In B K6. In A, K2, K2 tog (12
sts)

Row 26 – In A, P2 tog. In B, P8. In A, P2 tog, cutting
and tying A (10 sts)

Row 27 – In B, K2 tog, K6, K2 tog (8 sts)

Row 28 – In B, P8

Row 29 – In B K2 tog, K4, K2 tog (6 sts)

Row 30 – In B P2 tog, P2, P2 tog (4 sts)

Cast off.

Saucer
Cast on 21 sts

Row 1 – K
Row 2 – P, inc 1 st ea end (23 sts)
Row 3 – K, inc 1 st ea end (25 sts)
Row 4 – P, inc 1 st ea end (27 sts)
Row 5 – K, inc 1 st ea end (29 sts)
Row 6 – P
Row 7 – K2 tog, K to last 2 sts, K2 tog (27 sts)
Row 8 – P2 tog, P to last 2 sts, P2 tog (25 sts)
Row 9 – K2 tog, K to last 2 sts, K2 tog (23 sts)
Row 10 – P2 tog, P to last 2 sts, P2 tog (21 sts)
Cast off.

Teacup

(CC is coffee colour. All sts are to be worked in main colour unless CC is stated. Cut a length of about 20 cm (8 in) of main colour before you start, for use in row 15.)

Cast on 11 sts
Row 1 – K
Row 2 – P
Row 3 – K, inc 1 st ea end (13 sts)
Row 4 – P
Row 5 – K
Row 6 – P, inc 1 st ea end (15 sts)
Row 7 – Cast on 4 sts at beginning of row, K to end (19 sts)
Row 8 – P to last st, inc in last st (20 sts)
Row 9 – Inc in first st, K to end (21 sts)
Row 10 – Inc in first st, P15, P3 in CC, P1, M1, P1 (23 sts)
Row 11 – K2, K3 in CC, K to end
Row 12 – P18, P3 in CC, P2
Row 13 – K to last st, inc in last st (24 sts)
Row 14 – P to last st, P2 tog (23 sts)
Row 15 – Cast off 4 sts, K3, K13 in CC, K3 (for these last 3 sts you might want to use a separate length of main colour to avoid having to carry the main thread across the CC) (19 sts)
Row 16 – P2 tog, P15 in CC, P2 tog (17 sts)
Row 17 – K2 tog, K to last 2 sts, K2 tog (15 sts)
   Cast off purlwise. Make up as per the Union Jack bunting on page 80.

Hanging hearts

These folksy hearts can be stuffed with lavender to hang in your wardrobe, or you could keep them simply decorative. A string of three hearts hanging from a cupboard handle or on the back of a door would look pretty. I have included a grid for letters so you can spell out words or mark the initials of someone special. A bunting string with 'Dream', 'Sleep' or a baby's name would be beautiful for a nursery. I would recommend knitting a few plain hearts which can be used for backing before attempting intarsia letters if you are not confident with intarsia.

I used Rowan Cashsoft DK and Patons 100% Cotton DK. (See Shade chart on page 123 for details of colours.)

You will need

· · · · · · · · · · · · · ·

★ *DK yarn.*
★ *1 pair 4 mm (US #6) needles*
★ *Ribbon*
★ *A little toy stuffing*

Finished size

· · · · · · · · · · · · ·

★ *Approx. 12 cm x 14 cm (4.75 x 5.5 in) when*
  knitted in DK on 4 mm needles (US #6)

Note

· · · · ·

★ *The heart is worked from the top down. Each*
  separate 'hump' of the heart is worked first,
  then they are joined together.

Letters

If you are knitting the letters in, look at the grid showing the heart and lightly mark with a pencil where your chosen letter will be inside it. Start the letter pattern on row 7. We are working from the top down, so have a little think about which way round your letter will be and at which point to start it. Don't worry, if it sounds too complicated, an easier option is to knit the heart and add the letters later using the Swiss darning technique (see page 110).

If you choose to use intarsia, don't forget to twist the two strands of yarn when you change colour to prevent holes appearing.

To make the heart

Cast on 6 sts
Row 1 – K1, M1 (by knitting into the front and the back of loop), K to last st, M1, K1 (8 sts)
Row 2 – P1, M1 (by knitting purlwise into the back then the front of loop), P to last st, M1, P1 (10 sts)
Rows 3 and 4 – Repeat these first two rows once more (14 sts)

Row 5 – K1, M1, K to end (15 sts)

Cut yarn and leave these sts on the needle. Repeat from the beginning to form the second 'hump'. Cast on to the free needle

Row 6 – P 14 sts, then continuing from the first 'hump' onto the second, tying in the loose end from the first hump, P2 tog. P14 (29 sts)

Continue in st st without increasing for 6 more rows (29 sts)

Row 13 – K2 tog, K to last 2 sts, K2 tog (27 sts)

Row 14 – P

Repeat these two rows 3 times more (21 sts)

Row 21 – K2 tog, K to last 2 sts, K2 tog (19 sts)

Row 22 – P2 tog, P to last 2 sts, P2 tog (17 sts)

Continue decreasing 1 st at each end until only 3 sts remain.

Row 30 – P3 tog

Fasten off.

To make up

Make two to sew together and stuff, or draw around your knitted heart on fabric to create a template for a fabric backing. I have used an iron-on bonding fabric to fuse pink gingham to the back of the hanging hearts for the words 'Tea time'. This strengthens them and stops them from curling up.

Strawberry edging

Using the strawberries on page 32 you can make a pretty edging for a Roman blind, cushion or shelf edge. It would look beautiful around a Moses basket if you were lining a basket as a present, or would make a funky edging to a bag. You could work it all in fine crochet cotton on very small needles for a delicate miniature version.

The zig zag border alone would make a lovely edging for a window blind or café curtain worked in white or cream cotton and would look similar to a lace edging, especially if it were worked in fine crochet cotton on 2 mm needles.

Knit the zig zag edging for the length you need first, then count the 'points' of the zig zag edging to see how many strawberries you will need to make. You could replace the strawberries with the cherries from the cupcakes on page 29 to give a pompom border.

As this is worked in garter stitch, there is no right or wrong side, making it ideal for things like cushions where you may see both sides of the edging.

I knitted this all in 4-ply cotton, including the strawberries, but it would work just as well made in DK with 4 mm (US #6) needles, although it would obviously come up larger.

I used Patons 100% Cotton 4-ply. (See Shade chart on page 123 for details of colours.)

You will need

★ 4-ply or DK cotton. I used Patons 100% Cotton in 4-ply.
★ The amount you need will depend on how long your edging is to be, but unless you are making a vast amount, you should only need one ball for the edging plus all the necessary colours to make the strawberries
★ 3.25 mm (US #3) needles or 4 mm (US #6) needles if using DK
★ A little toy stuffing

Tension

★ One pattern repeat of 20 rows should be approximately 4 cm (1.5 in) in length when worked in 4-ply on 3.25 mm needles or 7 cm (2.75 in) in DK on 4 mm needles (US #6 or size you need to obtain correct tension). Knitting one pattern repeat for a tension test will give you an idea of how many repeats you will need to create your length of edging. If you work out that your desired length of edging will mean that you can't stop after row 20 of the pattern repeat, you may want to consider using larger or smaller needles so that you will be able to finish after row 20, although there is a certain amount of 'give' in the edging that means you can stretch it a little without losing its form.

Zig zag edging

Cast on 9 sts.
Edging row – K
Begin zig zag pattern:
Row 1 – K1, yo, {K2 tog, yo} twice, K4 (10 sts)
Row 2 (and all alternate rows) – K
Row 3 – K1, yo, {K2 tog, yo} twice, K5 (11 sts)
Row 5 – K1, yo, {K2 tog, yo} twice, K6 (12 sts)
Row 7 – K1, yo, {K2 tog, yo} twice, K7 (13 sts)
Row 9 – K1, yo, {K2 tog, yo} twice, K8 (14 sts)
Row 11 – {Sl 1, K1, PSSO, yo} x 3, Sl 1, K1, PSSO, K6 (13 sts)
Row 13 – {Sl 1, K1, PSSO, yo} x 3, Sl 1, K1, PSSO, K5 (12 sts)
Row 15 – {Sl 1, K1, PSSO, yo} x 3, Sl 1, K1, PSSO, K4 (11 sts)
Row 17 – {Sl 1, K1, PSSO, yo} x 3, Sl 1, K1, PSSO, K3 (10 sts)

Row 19 – {Sl 1, K1, PSSO, yo} x 3, Sl 1, K1, PSSO, K2 (9 sts)
Row 20 – K

Repeat these 20 rows until you have the desired
length of edging.

Techniques & templates

The next few pages will give you an idea of how to do some of the techniques I have used throughout the book. I have used contrasting colours to make it easier for you to see what I'm doing, but of course you will be using whatever colour you need for your design. I have also provided charts and templates for the designs I have used, but why not be brave and make up your own? Knitters' graph paper is readily available to download on the Internet.

Picking up stitches from rows below

Picking up stitches from a row several rows previous to the one you are working on will essentially fold that section of knitting in half and secure it.

I have knitted the row from which the stitches are to be picked up in red to make it easier to see.

1. Locate the stitch to be picked up. This will be in the same column of stitches as the one you are about to work.

3. Slip the stitch to be picked up onto your left needle.

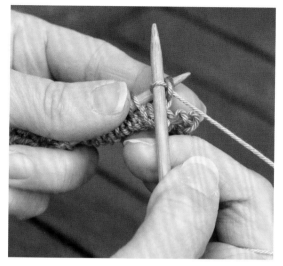

2. Insert the working needle into both the next stitch of your row and the stitch you have just picked up, knitting them both together as you would in a conventional 'K2 tog'.

4. Continue along the row, picking up each stitch from the row below as you have just done.

Finger-chained cord

This is useful for creating loops for buttonholes or a cord for making bows (as in the Tank top on page 62). If you know how to crochet, you will know how to do this with a hook, as it is simply a tight foundation chain. However, if you don't, you can make it easily with your fingers.

1. Make a slip knot.

2. Start to pull the long end through the loop of the slip knot, but don't pull it completely through, just enough to make another loop.

3. Holding onto the new loop you have just made, tighten the loop of the slip knot.

4. Start to pull the long end through the new loop, but again pull only enough through to make a new loop.

5. Tighten the loop you made in step 2 and repeat until you have enough cord, pulling new loops through the old loops and tightening the old loops.

Swiss darning

Swiss darning is a way to achieve an intarsia effect that enables you to create complex patterns or use many colours in a way that would be very difficult to achieve through intarsia. Basically, you are 'tracing' over the stitches that are already there in a different colour. It is really simple to do and looks very effective.

1. Thread a large darning needle with your yarn and sew through a stitch at the back to start off. I like to leave a long tail at this point and sew it in later, but you could knot the thread on the back to secure it.

2. Come through from the back of the knitting in the point of the 'V' of the stitch you are going to duplicate.

3. Put your needle in through the front of the fabric at the top right end of the 'V' and bring it up from the back to the front at the top left end of the 'V'.

4. Put your needle back through the bottom point of the 'V'. Pull through to the back.

5. You have completed your first stitch!

6. Continue to work the others in the same way. It is best to start at the bottom of a column of stitching and work your way up, going into the next stitch and the bottom point of the 'V' again.

Sewing edges together (mattress stitch)

I struggled for years with sewing edges together and always seemed to manage to have lumpy, unattractive seams. This method takes longer than oversewing but will result in a beautiful, neat edge.

1. Line up the two edges, A and B, right sides together. Fasten off your yarn at one end. Pick up the inside stitch from edge A and the inside stitch of edge B.

2. Take the needle back through edge B and through the corresponding stitch on edge A.

3. You will now go through the next inside stitch along on edge A, then through the corresponding inside stitch on edge B.

4. Repeat in this way along the length. If you have worked a lot of increases and decreases and your edges are untidy, roll the knitting slightly so you can get in to the next row of stitches in from the edge. Sew up through these as per the instructions above.

Blocking

If you have put a lot of effort into making a beautiful piece of knitting, especially if it's a garment, it's worth taking a bit more time to block it properly. I know you're probably desperate to make it up straight away, because I know I always am, but it will be worth a day's wait to finish it properly. There are lots of ways of blocking, which you can find on the Internet, but I am going to show you how I do it.

1. Lay a towel down straight onto a carpet if you have one, or any other surface you can stick pins into, a large sofa cushion or a bed you won't need to sleep in.

2. Lay your knitting out on the towel, check your measurements again and stretch it into the correct size and shape.

3. Pin around all the edges.

4. Spray with clean water. I have an empty spray bottle that I keep solely for this purpose. You don't need to completely soak your work, but make sure it's wet all over.

5. Wait until the knitting is completely dry, preferably overnight. Remove the pins.

Charts and templates

Little bird dress page 50

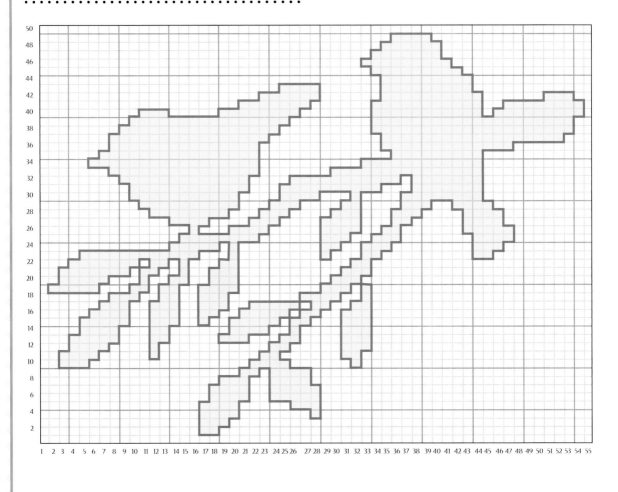

Bunting page 78

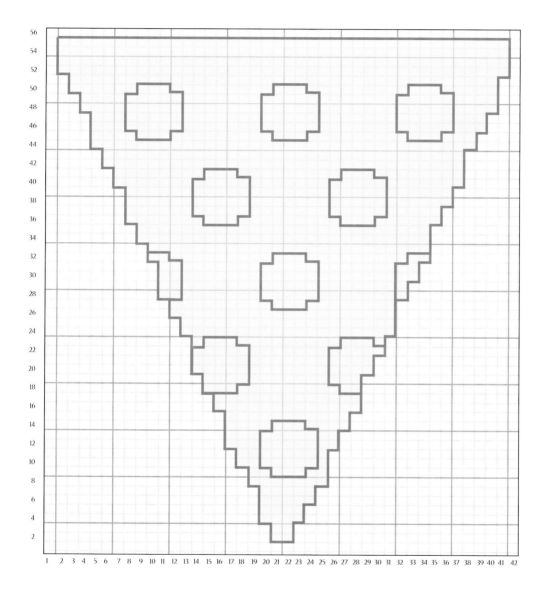

Alphabet page 96

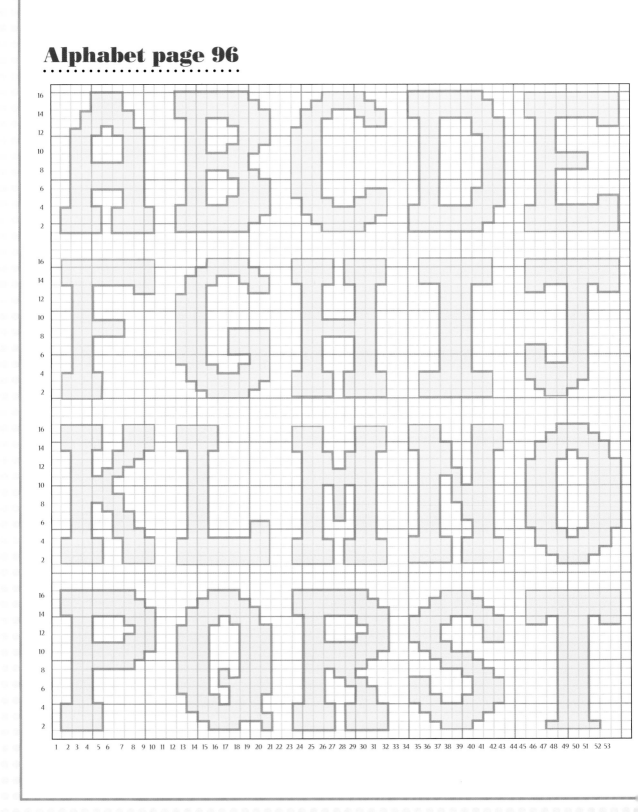

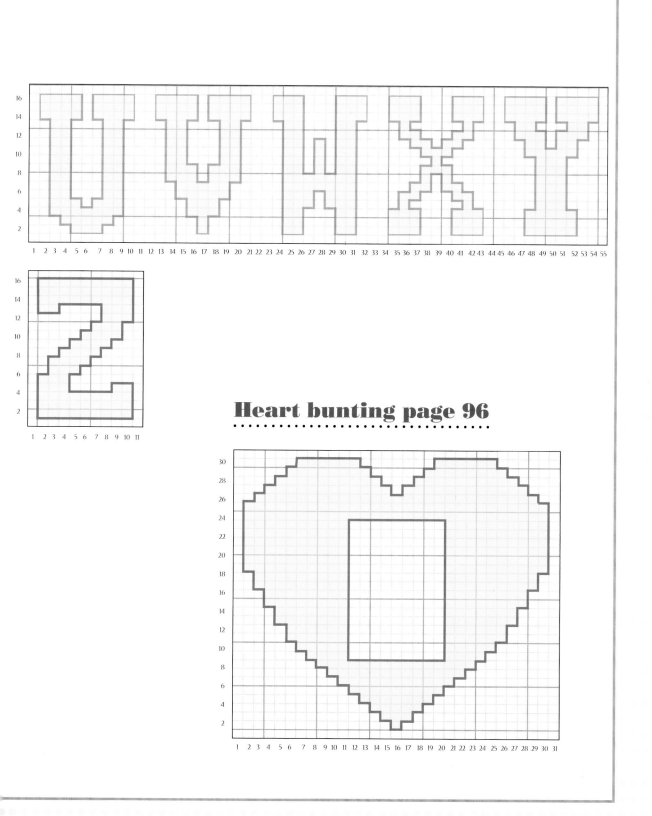

Heart bunting page 96

Numbers page 44

Templates are shown at 100%

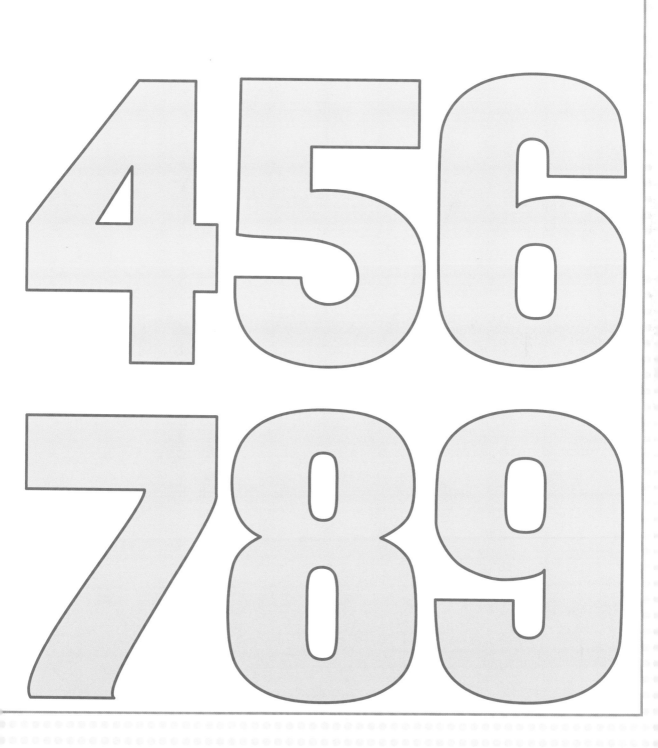

Pirate jumper page 44

Templates are shown at 100%

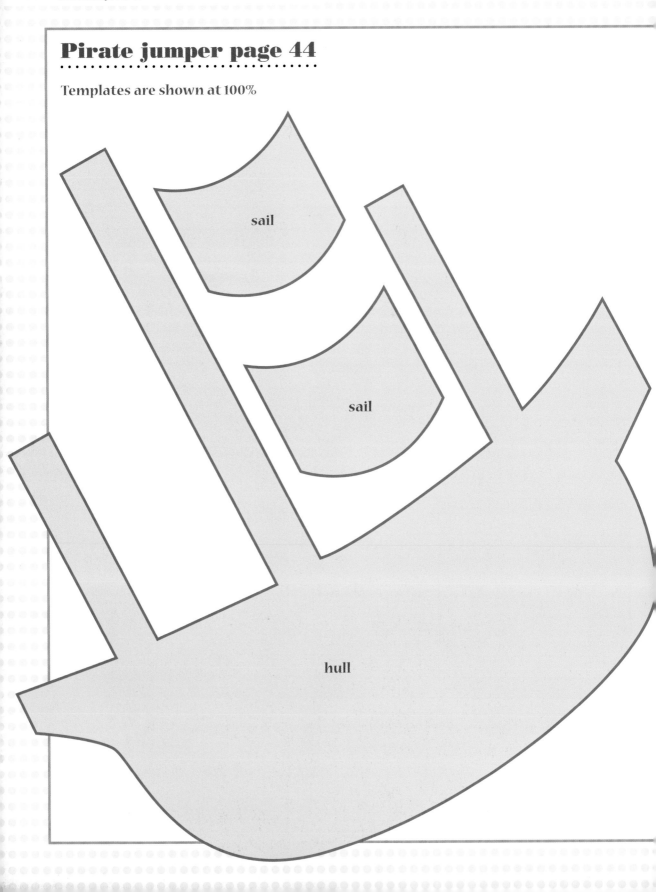

flag

mainsail

Glossary

UK	US
cast off	bind off
DK (double knitting)	lightweight
4-ply	superfine
moss stitch	seed stitch
stocking stitch	stockinette stitch
swiss darning	duplicate stitching
tension	gauge

Needle size conversion chart

Metric size	UK size	US size
2.0mm	14	0
2.25mm	13	1
2.75	12	2
3.0mm	11	-
3.25mm	10	3
3.5mm	-	4
3.75mm	9	5
4.0mm	8	6
4.5mm	7	7
5.0mm	6	8
5.5mm	5	9
6.0mm	4	10
6.5mm	3	10 $\frac{1}{2}$
7.0mm	2	-

Shade chart

Please note that where some of the shades have been replaced by the manufacturers, I have referenced the current shade. This means that some shades may differ from those shown in the photographs.

Fairy blossom tea set
Patons DK 100% Cotton
Denim 2697
Apple 2205

Plain tea set
Wendy Supreme Luxury Cotton DK
Sunflower 1922
Patons DK 100% Cotton
Pale blue 2173
Lilac 2701

Strawberries / Strawberry edging
Patons DK / 4-ply 100% Cotton
Red 2115/ 1115
Apple 2205/1205
Yellow 2740/1740

Stripy-sleeved sweaters:

Robot sweater
Patons 4-ply 100% Cotton
Sky 1702
Apple 1205
Kingfisher 1739
Pale Blue 1173

Est. 2012 sweater
Rowan 4-ply Cashsoft
Weather 425
Loganberry 430
Deep 431

Est. 2006 sweater
Patons 4-ply 100% Cotton
Cream 1692
Limestone 1716
Oak 1722

Pirate sweater
Patons 4-ply 100% Cotton
Red 1115
White 1691
Kingfisher 1739

Little bird dresses:

Red, white and blue dress
Patons 4-ply 100% Cotton
Red 1115
Cream 1692
Denim 1697

Pale blue dress
Patons 4-ply 100% Cotton
Sky 1702
Oak 1722

Age 7 dress
Patons 4-ply 100% Cotton
Nectarine 1723
Purple 1743

Stripy tank tops:

Boys' age 6–12 m
Baby Bamboo by Sirdar
Pale Brown 170
Willow 133
Cream 131
Pale blue 169

Boys' age 7–8
Patons DK 100% Cotton
Limestone 2716
Orchard 2721
Grape 2733

Girls' age 3–4
Patons DK 100% Cotton
Red 2115
Fuchsia 2742
Neroli 2741
Apple 2205

Girls' age 1–2
Patons DK 100% Cotton
Red 2115

Denim 2697
Cream 2692

Bow dresses:
Age 1–2
Fuchsia 1742
Purple 1743

Age 3–4
Nougat 1715
Bright Pink 1719

Girls' lacy shrug
Wendy Supreme Luxury Cotton
DK
Sunflower 1922

Ladies' lacy shrug
Patons DK 100% Cotton
Red 2115

Ladies' summer shrug
Patons 4-ply 100% Cotton
Jade 1726

Spot and stripe bunting
Baby Bamboo by Sirdar
Blue 169
Cream 131
Babe 134
Flip Flop 125
Limey 155

Union Jack bunting
Patons DK 100% Cotton
Denim 1697

Daisy chain
Patons 4-ply 100% Cotton
White 1691
Yellow 1740
Apple 1205

Knitted corsages
Patons DK 100% Cotton
Nougat 2715
Denim 2697
Red 2115

Cups and saucers bunting
Baby Bamboo by Sirdar
Pale Brown 170
Cream 131
Pale Blue 169

Hanging hearts
RYC Cashsoft by Rowan
Vamp 532
Rose 817 (Shade has been
replaced. An alternative would
be Sweet 501)
Cloud 805

Stockists

UK stockists

Beaker Button
Studio 11
Fairground Craft & Design Centre
Weyhill
Andover
Hampshire
SP11 0QN
+44 (0)7738 534164
www.beakerbutton.co.uk

Patons
Coats Crafts UK
Green Lane Mill
Holmfirth
West Yorkshire
HD9 2DX
+44 (0)1484 690803
www.coatscrafts.co.uk

Rowan Yarns
Green Lane Mill
Holmfirth
West Yorkshire
HD9 2DX
+44 (0)1484 681881
www.knitrowan.com

Sirdar Spinning Ltd.
Flanshaw Lane
Wakefield
West Yorkshire
WF2 9ND
+44 (0)1924 231669
www.sirdar.co.uk

Wendy Yarns
Thomas B Ramsden & Co. (Bradford) Ltd.
Netherfield Road
Guiseley
Leeds
LS20 9PD
+44 (0)1943 872264
www.tbramsden.co.uk

US stockists: see the store locator at www.knitrowan.com

Australian stockists

Sunspun
185 Canterbury Road
Canterbury
Victoria
3126
+61 (0)3 98301609
www.sunspun.com.au

The Wool Shack
+61 (0)8 93718864
www.woolshack.com

Yarn Over
1/265 Blaker Road
Keperra, Brisbane
Queensland
4054
+61 (0)7 38512608
www.yarnover.com.au

Acknowledgements

There are so many lovely people to thank for their help in producing this book. Firstly a very big thank you to Susan James who took a chance on me and to Agnes Upshall at Bloomsbury for making the idea become a reality. Thank you to the very talented Ella Mayfield for the stunning photographs. Without you Ella, there would be no book.

Thank you so much to my beautiful models: Olivia, Xenia, Zain, Sienna, Louis, Isaac, Gabriel, Jasper, Gabriella, Rosie and my gorgeous girls Esmé and Isla. You were all so well behaved and you look lovely.

A massive thank you to all the wonderful ladies who helped test the patterns: Tessa Senior, Anne Wolton, Celia Faulkner, Valerie Adcock, and Lianne Wright. Special thanks to Catherine Hall for the most perfect knitting I have ever seen; the ever-inspirational Ruth Lewendon, and to my wonderful and patient mother, Hazel Hawtin, who knitted up a storm helping me. You are all brilliant, thank you.

A big thank you to a big inspiration to me, Erika Knight, who gave me great advice on getting started, and to my father, Alistair Hawtin, for putting us in touch and sharing his own book-writing experience.

Many thanks are also due to Katie Battey and Sarah Brook at Coats Crafts, thank you so much, ladies.

Huge thanks to two more lovelies: Ann and Constance Sinclair provided amazing cakes and beautiful china for the photographs.

Thank you to the Tuesday Club members for keeping the tea and cakes coming and for listening to my moaning… And last but by no means least, a massive thank you to my fabulous husband Rupert for being my rock through this project and always.

★ Cupcakes by Mini Mama's Cakery at minimamascakery.co.uk
★ Photography by Ella Jane Mayfield at ellajanephotography.co.uk

Index